An Account
of the Things
# of Yucatán

Fray Diego de Landa

An Account of the Things of Yucatán

Written by the bishop of Yucatán, based on the oral traditions of the ancient Mayas

MONCLEM
EDICIONES

AN ACCOUNT OF THE THINGS OF YUCATAN

Translation: David Castledine
Illustrations: José Narro & Eraclio Ramírez
First edition: 2000
Fifth reprint: 2009
Copyright © by Monclem Ediciones, S.A. de C.V.
Leibnitz 31, Col. Anzures 11590 México, D.F.
monclem@monclem.com
Tel.: 52 55 47 67
Printed in Mexico
Impreso en México
ISBN 978-970-9019-02-5

Contents

Introduction

Diego de Landa has been considered a contradictory man and a fanatical, intolerant friar. According to a portrait from the time, he had a grim, even threatening look, with deep circles under his eyes, pointed nose, cleft chin and broad forehead. In character he was said to be rash, violent and impetuous, which in the long run led him to commit imprudent, inhuman and cruel acts against the Mayas.

Historians who have examined his life and this work say that he was a typical Western man, or rather a man influenced by the ethos of the Renaissance, to explain his behavior and particularly why on the one hand he destroyed articles, codices and monuments that were obstacles to the implantation of Christian doctrine in the Maya region, while on the other he collected and arranged data about the history and customs of the group to later produce his manuscript of the Relación de las Cosas de Yucatán (Account of the Things of Yucatán) where he gives a complete record of ancient Maya culture. Some experts have judged this work as simply an apologia or a way of freeing his conscience of the evil he had done, and others as one of the most valuable documents on the Mayas, indispensable for the study of one of the greatest cultures in pre-Hispanic America.

Although there is not much information about his life, he is known to have been born in Cifuentes, Alcarria, in the old kingdom of Toledo, in 1524. He entered the Franciscan order at the age of 17 at the convent of San Juan de los Reyes de Toledo and was later ordained as a priest. The next news about him is when he arrived in Yucatán in 1549 as a member of the mission organized by brother Nicolás de Albalate.

When the Conquest was only just over, the colony of New Spain began to be established and there were still groups of rebellious Mayas. Yucatán was organized as a political and territorial unit, with the object of distributing the land and its inhabitants or impoing the *encomienda* system (grants of Indian villages, their inhabitants and land) for the benefit of colonists. This system used native labor at will without any pay or remuneration in exchange. Abuses were also common, such as forced personal service by the Indians in the homes of Spaniards and high taxes.

The year Landa arrived in Yucatán several thousand pesos had been collected in taxes, and numbers of Indians had been persecuted. Because of this, many fled, seeking refuge in the hills and isolated areas. Therefore the missionaries, whose lives were also dependent on native labor, joined the conquistadors to ensure they returned. The tactics used by the friars were more fruitful, since they were able to persuade the Indians to go back to the villages, and in this way they could begin evangelization and at the same time control their work force more effectively.

So as to do their work properly, missionaries went through a stage of preparation; when they arrived in Yucatán they studied the Mayan language using a grammar written by friar Luis de Villalpando as their textbook. Once they had mastered the language, they could communicate, teach Christian doctrine and understand native life. Then they left for different areas to undertake the spiritual conquest of the population. Thus, their task had several purposes: to wean the Indians from pagan practices, convert them to Christianity and obtain their submission.

They were only completely triumphant in the last of these, since the indians accepted and practiced the new faith only in appearance, but in private continued to worship their ancient deities. This was because the friars did not achieve real acculturation, since it was to their advantage to keep the Indians ignorant of the knowledge possessed by the Spanish civilization to make them as productive as possible in their work.

The friars helped to provide Indians for the *encomenderos* (holders of *encomiendas*) for whom they had to work in the fields and perform a wide range of manual tasks. But soon, because of the heavy taxes imposed by the encomenderos which considerably reduced what corresponded to the friars, both groups began a struggle for the monopoly of wealth.

At the time, there was a dispute about the spiritual and moral position of the Indians, a consequence of which was the protectionist policy decreed by the Crown. Judge Tomás López went to Yucatán and with his Ordinances laid the foundations for the peaceful coexistence of the conquistadors and the conquered. In addition, mestizos now entered on the scene, who instead of forming a bridge between the two groups were looked down on and also kept apart from Spanish culture, as they were only accepted as stewards, laborers or specialized artisans. But they had other problems too: economic difficulties and a conflict of ethnic identification.

It was a time of great paradoxes, disputes and reconciliation in which the two cultures confronted each other and clashed violently to be able to adapt. The period coincided with the arrival of Diego de Landa, and some scholars surmise that all this may have had an influence on his later behavior. As was the rule in his order, he devoted the first years of his stay to the intensive study of the Maya language, as well as going through a period of adjustment to a life of material privations and of adaptation to a new concept of the world in the spiritual sense, finding himself in a human and natural environment very different from the one he knew.

When he could speak the language fluently, he began to travel all over the peninsula to convert the inhabitants of different communities and observe their customs and way of life. Three years later, in 1552, he was appointed guardian of the convent of Izamal, due to his knowledge of local culture. There he began to show some aspects of his character, since in exchange for his services he managed to hoard a large quantity of corn which afterwards, in times of shortage, he bartered for the work of the inhabitants of Izamal in an improvement project.

During the period he devoted to evangelizing there were other indications of his intolerance and severity. When he was assigned the task of converting the Indians in the region of Yokultz, he learned of an idolatrous celebration and immediately presented himself there, showed a cross and spoke about its power, and thus was able to halt the gathering. In Dzitas he was informed of another festival of this type and quickly arrived to break vessels and destroy idols.

The evangelical zeal with which he pursued his activities earned him the post of Prelate Custodian of the province in 1556. At this time, the natives began to flee their villages again because of excessive demands, leaving the friars without funds. Landa vented his anger on the *encomenderos*, censuring various sins, especially the practice of keeping concubines, with the object of forcing them to hand over the part corresponding to the order derived from the exploitation of the natives. However, he was prepared to overlook these sins if they gave his order a portion of the revenues.

As the *encomenderos* took no notice, Landa stripped the regular clergy of the highest earning parishes, causing a serious schism between the friars and the clergy and between these two parties and the *encomenderos*. Because of these problems, he decided to go to Guatemala City, then capital of the province, to lodge a complaint before the Court of Appeals (*Audiencia*). This body decreed that he should be accompanied by the Royal Inspector (*Visitador*) Jufre de Loaysa, who reviewed the situation personally and gave instructions for tax, which was handed over to the Crown and the *encomenderos*, to be reduced, Shortly afterward, Landa sent brother Lorenzo de Bienvenida to Spain to arrange the formation of a provincialship which would facilitate the freedom of action of missionaries vis-à-vis the regular clergy. But when the decision arrived in 1560, Landa could not pretend to the post because he was already guardian of the Great Convent of Mérida.

This same year, basing himself on the privileges granted to his order by popes Leo X, Adrian VI and Paul III, affirming that the members of religious orders had special powers to impose authority when there was no episcopal one. Landa extended them to include Inquisition. He judged it advantageous to handle an instrument like the Holy Office with the object of both inspiring fear in the *encomenderos* and abolishing idolatry. As prelate custodian he instigated various trials records of which can be found today in files of the Inquisition in the National Archives.

The activities of native priests continued alive among the indigenous population, since although outwardly cults no longer existed, the beliefs, rituals and deities of their ancient culture survived clandestinely. Landa must have known this perfectly well, in view of his life among the natives and knowledge of the inhabitants.

Brother Francisco de la Torre replaced Landa as custodian prelate, and during his period of office, authorization was given to create the ecclesiastical province, and in December 1561, Landa was appointed provincial, with both the convents of Yucatán and Guatemala under his authority. At that time, the place was under district governor (*alcalde mayor*) Diego de Quixada who, using his position and other means, abused Indian labor for his personal benefit and also had agreements with former French pirates for commercial transactions. The governor's position was difficult: he had had a disagreement with Landa in which the latter had been understanding; he was at loggerheads with the *encomenderos* over economic issues and angry with the members of the municipal council because they did not intercede with the Crown for him to be given a higher rank and salary. Out of fear of the friar¥s growing power, he preferred to ally himself with him.

The exact date is not known with any certainty, but it is said to have been in June 1562 when two young Indian men, according to one source, or the gatekeeper of Maní convent, according to others, discovered small clay idols and skulls in a cave and reported this to the brothers of the convent. They were asked to bring some examples and after examining them, brother Pedro de Ciudad Rodrigo, the guardian, had several Indians apprehended and by torture made them confess that they did indeed have more idols in their homes and held ceremonies for them.

The provincial, Landa, was notified immediately, He talked with the district governor, asking him to provide constables and with them went to Maní. At the same time, he sent other friars, accompanied by guards to nearby villages including Yaxkab·, Zotuta, Canchunup and Homun with orders to apprehend all Indians suspected of practicing idol worship. Arriving at their appointed destinations, the friars proceeded to detain Indians and in some places carried out public acts of inquisition.

The most notorious or impressive was the one in Maní, at which the district governor, Quixada, the provincial, Landa, brother Miguel de la Puebla, brother Juan Pizarro and brother Pedro de Ciudad Rodrigo were present, who acted as inquisitors. Those accused, bound with ropes, wearing *corozas* (cone-shaped paper caps which were placed on the heads of captives as a humiliation), and naked from the waist up, were led in procession, accompanied by canticles, to the royal standard and the flags of the Holy Office. Many were punished with personal service in Spanish households, some were tortured, others whipped, had their heads shaven, or else they were made to wear a sanbenito (a conical hat worn by penitents reconciled with the Holy Office).

Many Indians, on seeing that those who declared themselves guilty were not tortured, also confessed, thus adding to the group which were given punishments. With the fines imposed, the auto-da-fé brought the friars revenues in both gold and cacao beans. Many idols, large stones used as altars, a wide variety of small sculptures and vessels of different sizes were destroyed, and codices with hieroglyphs painted on deerskin were burned.

The auto-da-fé of Manì caused great disturbance and indignation in the region, particularly among the *encomenderos* who were hostile to Landa and Quixada. Also, because many Indians were in prison, their was a shortage of labor and they were afraid that the fields would be abandoned and the province struck by famine. Meanwhile, the Indians became surly and distrustful, so much so that a rebellion was suspected, since the native caciques who tried to free their subjects in Mérida were also imprisoned by the Franciscans, and this provoked even greater anger in the population.

It was then that they heard about the landing of Francisco Toral in Campeche, who had been elected bishop shortly before. Landa went to see him immediately, but the bishop had already asked the Defender of the Indians, Diego Rodríguez de Vivanco, for details about the auto-da-fé of Maní, and began to take steps to curtail any interference in matters that were exclusively his area of responsibility.

Toral wrote to the king to accuse Landa and Quixado, informing him that "instead of doctrine the Indians received torture, and instead of helping them to know God, they make them despair, and the most tragic thing was that they asserted that without these punishments they could not teach divine law." He also proceeded to free the imprisoned Indians, abolished the personal services of those who had been punished in this way, and took the sanbenitos away.

However, Landa did not give up, He preached in contradiction to the bishop, kept the Indians excommunicated and even forbade their Christian burial. But all this trouble died down when Landa went to Spain in 1542, either voluntarily or because he had been summoned. Later, the *encomenderos* wrote to the king that of the four friars who had participated and belonged to the Holy Office, signing themselves inquisitors, they knew that Landa and de la Puebla had left for Spain, but Pedro de Ciudad Rodrigo had stayed for a time in Havana, waiting for the opportunity to sail, while brother Juan de Pizarro was in

Guatemala. Furthermore, the Indians were requesting the monarch that Landa and his colleagues do penance for all the harm they had caused which they would always remember and would tell future generations about so that this injustice would remain in the memory of the group.

Before leaving Yucatán, Landa was still trying to stir up trouble for Bishop Toral. In Spain, the king handed the bishop's accusations over to the Council of the Indies, whose members severely criticized him for having assumed the functions of bishop and inquisitor. Landa defended himself by arguing that his order had been given this authority by Pope Adrian VI, which caused even greater displeasure among the Council members. They decided to send him, together with his allegations and the bishop's accusations, to brother Pedro de Bobadilla, the provincial of Castile, but because of health problems, he in turn sent them to brother Pedro Guzm·n, who was recognized for his experience in matters of the Inquisition. Also, opinions were requested from seven learned scholars of the kingdom of Toledo, some of whom had been in America as judges or royal inspectors, and others were university professors of canon law, the Holy Scriptures or theology. These men finally passed judgement that both the auto-da-fé and the punishments meted out to the Indians had been lawful and in order.

Landa himself later remarked that the verdict had been absolvent, but his prolonged stay in Spain and the fact that the Council of the Indies did not send Bishop Toral any recommendations or comments about having freed the Indians leads to the conclusion that they agreed with his action. Landa had not been forgotten In Yucatán and still had loyal friends and very bitter enemies. Therefore, he began a slow strategy with letters to his friends and, as a result, in 1567 the friars persuaded or forced some native chieftains to ask the king to send more of them and in particular to authorize Landa's return. The petition was refused.

Diego de Landa spent some time in the convent of Ocaño, then in the one of Guadalajara, in San Juan de los Reyes de Toledo, and later in San Antonio de Cabrera, where he held the post of guardian, so his stay in Spain stretched out to ten years, During this time, perhaps out of nostalgia for the distant Indies, or else plagued by memories, he decided to relate what he had experienced, learned and destroyed there.

So he wrote *Account of the Things of Yucatán* to satisfy a personal desire or to tell others about the customs and his knowledge of the Mayas. Thus he created a work on the culture that he himself had helped to destroy by burning the codices containing a large part of its heritage.

When Bishop Toral died in 1572, King Philip II of Spain appointed Landa to the bishopric of Yucatán, which he did in October 1573. The historian Justo Sierra O'Reilly remarks that he obtained this appointment through intrigue, as due to his hard, fanatical character he must have used influences and important recommendations to obtain the seat.

When he reached the province once again, the fears and grudges of the Indians and *encomenderos* were aroused, but Landa began his job calmly. He did try to withdraw the service of Indians as porters, but the governor and colonists objected and he did not take any action against them so as to avoid any trouble with the Crown. Later, when he learned that idolatrous acts were being performed in Campeche he did not go personally but sent father Fuente Ovejuna, who apprehended those guilty and had them whipped and their heads sheared, despite royal letters patent forbidding members of religious orders to take these measures. The Indian chieftain of the area, on advice from the *encomenderos*, lodged a complaint with the Royal Tribunal of New Spain, which demanded Landa's strict compliance and also told the governor, Velázquez de Gijón, not to tolerate this conduct from the friars, which was encouraging.

The Holy Office invited the bishop to attend the first auto-da-fé in New Spain, and he accepted in a letter dated March 22, 1574. Late the same year or early the following one he traveled to Mexico City and took the opportunity to have a catechism in the Maya language printed. There is little information about his other activities on this journey, but he is known to have visited Tabasco on his return and converted, not without some coercion, some sorcerers who were unwilling to do this spontaneously.

The disagreements and arguments continued because in the town of Peto the bishop's lay assistant went in pursuit of a native sorcerer who while being held in Chancenote was helped by the mayor of Valladolid to escape. Extremely angered by this, Landa excommunicated the mayor. The bishop then set off on a pastoral tour in the east of the peninsula. The mayor notified the governor who with his troops went to find him in Sitilpech, where they had a heated argument. Because of this, Landa complained to the court, and in a letter the king ordered the governor to maintain good relations with the bishop and cooperate with him. Landa tried to assume the role of inquisitor again, for which he was censured by the Tribunal of Mexico City and so stopped. He began to have problems with Diego de Santillán, the new governor of the province, but he now could do little, although his violent character prompted him to, since he was in delicate health. He died in Mérida on April 29, 1579 at the age of 55.

This book, as noted earlier, was written during the years Landa spent in Spain awaiting the verdict on his actions at Maní. He is assumed to have produced it for those who protected him and were concerned about his fate, but it is not known whether it bore any particular dedication. When the manuscript was finished and could have been printed, the author decided against it. So, when he returned to Yucatán as second bishop in 1573, he took the manuscript with him, and after his death it was kept in the archives of the Franciscan convent of Mérida. The *Relación de Chunchuchu y Tabí*, produced around 1581, makes a reference to the work, though it is not known whether it refers to the original in Mérida or a copy that may have remained in Spain. Also, several copies are said to have been made to be sent to Spain.

In time, other historians used Landa's manuscript as a source of information to include in their works, for example brother Diego de Cogolludo y Vázquez de Espinosa. There is no indication of when the original manuscript was lost, but it has been suggested that when the friars were expelled from Yucatán in 1820 one of them took it away. The work lay forgotten until 1863 when the abbé Brasseur de Bourbourg discovered it and published the first edition: *"Relation des Choses de Yucatán* by Diego de Landa, a text in Spanish and a translation into French, containing the signs of the calendar and the hieroglyphic alphabet of the Maya language accompanied by various historical and chronological documents, with a grammar and short French-Maya vocabulary, preceded by an essay on the ancient sources of Mexico and Central America; by the abbé Brasseur de Bourbourg, former ecclesiastical administrator of the Indians of Rabinal (Guatemala), member of the scientific commission of Mexico. Paris, Artus Bertrand, publisher; London, Trübner and Co., 1864."

The manuscript is now in the library of the Academia de Historia in Madrid. It is well-preserved, with legible writing; only proper names present a certain degree of difficulty because some letters can be confused with others. Landa's work bears the title of *Relación*, which at the time meant allegation, report and story: allegation because it contained arguments that must be known in order to be able to judge; report because it gives news and facts; history because it relates and describes. It puts Landaís arguments before the king and the Council of the Indies, offers evidence in his defense, and brings to light all he saw and knew during his time in Yucatán.

It begins with a description of the region, its geography and the meaning of its name. It refers to the ancient history of the Mayas, to Spanish expeditions and conquest, also highlighting the arrival of the Franciscans and Landa himself.

The book continues with a description of dwellings, means of subsistence, clothing and personal adornments, food and drink, agriculture and seeds, trade and currency. Following this, it gives references to arithmetic or way of counting, genealogies, inheritance, marriage, the way infants were named, the duties of priests, and sacrifices.

It goes on with war, military leaders, the punishment of adulterers, murderers and thieves; upbringing and education, death, funeral customs and the belief in an afterlife.

Then follows the most important section, which deals with the Yucatecan year count, the characters of the days considered inauspicious. The sacrifices made at the beginning of each year according to the letter that designated them. The book explains the calendar the Mayas used and compares it to the Roman one, tells of the Maya "century" and how it was shown in their characters. It closes with details of buildings, agricultural production and the flora and fauna of the region.

One of the most important merits of the *Relación*, apart from precise information about customs, religion, Mayan history and details of the Conquest is the insight into chronological glyphs which led to the decipherment of important dates in the history of this civilization.

The sources Landa used for his work were principally oral, obtained from conquistadors and Indians descended from the Xiu, Cocom and Chel tribes —in other words from living people— direct, reliable sources, the codices he later destroyed and his own keen observation.

The only written source the author refers to is Oviedo's *Historia General de las Indias*, but students of his work think that he must have read the book by López de Gómara *Historia de las Indias y Conquista de México* as well as writings by brother Bartolomé de las Casas on the West Indies. They also point out that it shows similarities with *Relación sobre las costumbres de los indios* by H'Chiu Xiu, who on being baptized took the name of Gaspar Antonio Herrera.

Landa did something similar to what brother Bernardino de Sahag'n had done years before, though it appears that he had no intention of writing a history. However, circumstances obliged him to, since what he wrote would serve as a defense against the accusations leveled at him by making public all the experiences stored up in his memory, which must have been exceptional, to retain so many, many details, It is definitely a narration written by an eye witness, a description that combines the attractiveness of tradition and the qualities of an ancient document.

To close, and at the same time underline the importance of the work, there follows the opinion given by one of the foremost investigators of Maya culture, J. Eric S. Thompson, in his book *The Rise and Fall of Maya Civilization* (1954: 34-35).

"Most important of these was Bishop Diego de Landa's history of Yucatán, written about 1560, a mine of information on Maya customs, religious beliefs, and history, together with a quite detailed account of the Maya calendar, illustrated with drawings of the glyphs. This was the indispensable foundation on which to reconstruct Maya hieroglyphic writing, and is as close to a Maya Rosetta stone as we are ever likely to get. Indeed, without this book it is doubtful whether we would have made any progress in glyph decipherment, and we would know very much less about the Maya. Bishop Landa, then a Franciscan friar, who reached Yucatán a few years after the Spanish Conquest, was a man of unquestionable ability. He has been much criticized for his severity in stamping out recrudescences of paganism, but in that he merely reflected the views of his century;... Landa, like any modern ethnologist, obtained his material from native informants. Oddly enough, had he not campaigned so violently against Maya relapses into paganism, we might not now have this prime source, for it was while he was in Spain, awaiting trial on charges of exceeding his authority, that he whipped his material into shape to serve as indirect testimony for the defense."

An Account of the Things of Yucatán, taken from the writings of Fray Diego de Landa of the Franciscan Order.

I

Description of Yucatan
The various seasons

Yucatan is not an island or even a point entering the sea as some people have thought, but mainland. They were deceived by either the Cape of Cotoche that the sea forms as it enters the Golfo Dulce through Ascension Bay, and by the headland on the side towards Mexico that is formed by the Desconocida, before it reaches Campeche, or by the extensive lagoons created near Puerto Real and Dos Bocas.

The land is very flat and free of mountains and so is not visible from ships until they are very close inshore except between Campeche and Champotón, where some low hills and a headland called Morro de los Diablos can be made out.

The course from Veracruz via Cape Catoche to Yucatán is less than 20° degrees, and via the mouth at Puerto Real, over 23 degrees. From one cape to the other must be some 130 leagues in a straight line.

The coastline is low, and so large vessels stay at some distance from land. The coast is also foul, full of rocks and reefs that wear at ships' cables severely, but there is a lot of mud, so that even if ships capsize near the shore few lives are lost.

At low tide the sea falls so much, especially in the Bay of Campeche, that often half a league is left dry in some places. These tides leave small fish in the ooze, mud and pools, on which many people live.

A range of low hills runs across Yucatan from corner to corner that begins near Champotón and ends at the town of Salamanca in the corner opposite. This range divides Yucatan into two parts; the southern area, towards Lacandón and Taíza is uninhabited since there is no water, except when it rains. The northern part is settled.

This land is very hot and the sun burns, although there are cooling breezes from the northeast or the one from the east that often blows, and in the afternoons, a breeze off the sea.

The people of this country live a long time, and there have been individuals aged one hundred and forty.

Winter begins on St. Francis' day [October 4] and lasts to the end of March, as this is when the north winds blow and causes the people to suffer from heavy colds and high fevers because of their scanty clothing. In late January and in February there is a short period of hot, sunny weather, and it does not rain at this time, except at new moon. The rains start in April and last until September; this is when the people sow all their crops, which ripen although it rains constantly. They sow a certain type of maize around St. Francis' day that is harvested after only a short time.

II

Etymology of the province's name. Its position

In the language of the Indians, this province is called *Ulumil cutz yetel ceh*, which means *Land of Turkeys and Deer*. They also called it *Petén*, meaning *Island*, being misled by the inlets and bays that have been mentioned.

When Francisco Hernández de Córdoba reached this country and landed at the point he named Cape Catoche he found some Indian fishermen and asked them what land it was. They replied *cotoch*, which means 'our houses' and 'our homeland' and this is why he gave the cape that name. When he asked them by signs by what right it was theirs they answered *ciuthan*, meaning *so they say*, and because of this the Spanish named it Yucatán. This was learned from one of the old conquistadors, Blas Hernández, who accompanied Governor Montejo the first time.

In the south part of Yucatán are the *Taiza* rivers and the Lacandon hills, and in the southwest lies the province of Chiapas. To reach Chiapas four rivers must be crossed that run dow from the mountains and join others to make the San Pablo and San Pedro, discovered by Grijalva in Tabasco. In the west are Xicalango and Tabasco, which form a single province.

Between the province of Tabasco and Yucatán are the two mouths where the sea breaks through. The larger of them is one league wide, but the other is not very large. The sea races in through these openings so furiously that is creates a great lagoon teeming with all sorts of fish and studded with so many small islands that the Indians mark the trees so as to find their way as they come and go in their boats between Tabasco and Yucatán. These islets, their shores and beaches are full of such a wide variety of seabirds that it is a wonderful and beuatiful sight. There is also a marvellous amount of game in the form of deer, rabbits, native pigs, and also monkeys, which do not live in Yucatán; there is also an amazing number of iguanas. On one of the islands stands the town of *Tixchel*.

The island of Cuba lies to the north, with Havana directly in front at 60 leagues distance; a little nearer is a small island belonging to Cuba called the Isle of Pines. To the east lies Honduras, and between this country and Yucatán the sea forms a great inlet that Grijalva named Ascension Bay. This is so full of islets that ships go off course among them, in particular those that trade between Yucatán and Honduras. Some 15 years ago a ship carrying many passengers and goods lost its way and when it went down all aboard it were drowned except a certain Majuelas and four others, who clung to a length of mast. And so they floated for three or four days without being able to reach any of the islets, until they all drowned through lack of strength except Majuelas. He was washed ashore half dead but regained strength by eating small conches and clams. Then he sailed from the island to the mainland on a raft that he made as well as the could from branches. On land, he was searching the coast for food when he found a crab but it clipped his thumb off at he top joint, causing him intense pain. Unsure of anything he set out through difficult country towards Salamanca, and when night fell he climbed a tree from where he saw a large tiger [jaguar] lie in wait for and then kill a deer; next morning he ate what remained.

Acros from Cape Catoche in Yucatán, but a little lower, is Cuzmil [Cozumel], separated from it by a channel five leagues wide between the mainland and this island, where the sea runs very high. Cusamil is an island fifteen leagues long and five leagues wide where only a few Indians live who speak the same language and have the same customs as those in Yucatán. The island lies on latitude 20.

Isla de Mujeres is thirteen leagues to the south of Cape Catoche and two leagues off the mainland, facing *Ekab*.

III

Captivity of Gerónimo de Aguilar. The expeditions of Hernández de Cordoba and Grijalva to Yucatán.

The first Spaniards to come to Yucatán are said to have been Gerónimo de Aguilar, a native of Ecija and his companions. In 1511, when there was trouble in the Darien because of the rivalry between Diego de Nicuesa and Vasco Nuñez de Balboa, these men followed Valdivia, who was sailing to Santo Domingo in a caravel to report to the admiral and governor about what was happening and to deliver 20,000 ducats due to the king. As it neared Jamaica, this caravel foundered on the Víboras sandbanks and sank. Only twenty men survived, who with Valdivia, escaped in a small boat without sails and only wretched oars, in which they were at sea for thirteen days withourt any food and water at all. After almost half of them had died of starvation, the others reached the coast of Yucatán, in a province called that of Maya, from where the language of Yucatán takes its name *Mayathan,* meaning *the language of Maya.*

These poor men fell into the hands of a bad chieftain who sacrificed Valdivia and four others to their idols then feasted his people on their flesh. He left Aguilar, Guerrero and five or six others to be fattened, but they broke down their prison and escaped into some hills. They found another chief, who was an enemy of the first and more merciful; he made use of them as slaves. The successor of this chief also treated them fairly, but they all died of sickness except Gerónimo de Aguilar and Gonzalo Guerrero. Of the two, Aguilar was a good

Francisco Hernández de Córdoba's 1517 expedition to the coast of Yucatán.

Christian and had a book of hours by which he knew the feast days. He escaped when the Marquis Hernán Cortés came in 1519. As Guerrero now knew the language he went to *Chectemal* (Chetumal), which is the Salamanca of Yucatán, and was there received by a chief called *Nachancàn* who put him in charge of warfare. He was very good at this, defeating his master's enemies many times and teaching the Indians how to fight and build fortresses and defenses. By this, and by living like an Indian, he earned a great reputation and they married him to a woman of very high rank, by whom he had children. Because of all this he never tried to escape as Aguilar had done; on the contrary, he tattooed his body, grew his hair long and pierced his ears so as to wear ornaments like the Indians, and it is likely that he became a worshiper of idols like them.

In Lent 1519, Francisco Hernández de Córdoba left Santiago de Cuba with three ships to seize slaves for the mines, since people were growing scarce in Cuba. Others say that he set out to discover new lands. With Alaminos as his pilot, he reached Isla de Mujeres, to which he gave this name because of the idols he found there of the country's goddesses such as *Aixchel*, *Ixchebeliax*, *Ixbunic* and *Ixbunieta*, who had skirts from the waist down and their breasts covered in the fashion of the Indian women. The building was stone, which surprised them and they found some gold objects, which they took. They reached Cape Catoche, rounded it into the bay of Campeche, and landed there on Lazarus Sunday, so naming it Lazarus. They were welcomed by the chief, and the Indians were amazed to see the Spaniards, touching their beards and bodies.

At Campeche they found a building in the sea, just off the coast, that was square and all in steps. At the top there was an idol with two ferocious animals devouring his sides, and a long, fat, stone serpent swallowing a lion. The animals were covered in blood from sacrifices. In Campeche they learned that there was a large town nearby, which was Champotón, and when they arrived found out that the chief was called *Mochcovoch*, a war-loving man who threw his people against the Spaniards. This weighed deeply on Francisco Hernández, as he saw how it must finish but, so as not to show less spirit, he placed his men in position and ordered guns fired from the ship. Although the noise, smoke and fire of the shots were new to the Indians, they nevertheless attacked with loud cries. The Spaniards fought back, inflicting terrible wounds and killing many. However, the chief roused the Indians so much that they forced the Spaniards to retreat, killing twenty, wounding fifty and taking two alive whom they later sacrificed. Francisco Hernández came out of this with thirty-three wounds, and thus returned sadly to Cuba, where he reported that the land was very good and rich because of the gold he had found on the Isla de Mujeres.

The news excited Diego Velásquez, the governor of Cuba and, many others, and he sent his nephew, Juan de Grijalva with four ships and two hundred men. With him went Francisco de Montejo, owner of one of the ships, and they set sail on May 1, 1518.

They took the same pilot, Alaminos, with them and arrived at the island of Cuzmil (Cozumel), from where the pilot sighted Yucatán. The other time, with Francisco Hernández, he had followed the right-hand coast southward, so now he decided to sail round it, if it was in fact an island, and veered left, continuing through the bay they named Ascension because they entered it that day. They sailed right round the coast until they reached Champotón once more, where they were taking on water when one man was killed and fifty wounded, among them Grijalva, who was hit by two arrows and had a tooth and a half broken.

So, they sailed away, naming the anchorage *Puerto de la Mala Pelea*. On this voyage they discovered New Spain, Pánuco and Tabasco, taking five months. They tried to land at Champotón, but the Indians resisted them so zealously that they approached close to the caravels in their canoes to loose their arrows at them. Therefore, they hoisted sails and left.

When Grijalva returned from his voyage of discovery and slave-trading in Tabasco and Ulúa, the great captain Hernán Cortés was in Cuba. When he heard the news of so much land and such wealth he desired to see them and even to win them for God and for his king; for himself and for his friends.

IV

Expedition of Cortés to Cozumel. A letter to Aguilar and his companions.

Cortés sailed out of Cuba with eleven ships, of which the largest was of one hundred tons, and placed eleven captains in them, he being one of them. He took 500 men, some horses and goods to trade, Francisco de Montejo, and the same Alaminos as chief pilot of the fleet. On his flagship he flew a banner with blue and white rays in honor of Our Lady, whose image he always placed together with the cross wherever he removed idols. On the banner there was a red cross with a legend around it that read *Amici sequamur crucem, et si habuerimos fidem in hoc signo vincemus.*

With this fleet and nothing more he set sail and reached Cozumel with ten ships because the other was separated from them in a storm but afterwards recovered on the coast. Their landfall on Cozumel was in the north, where they found fine stone buildings for the idols and a fair town, but the people there, on seeing so many ships and the soldiers disembarking, all ran away into the countryside.

Reaching the town, the Spaniards plundered it and settled themselves. As they were searching for people in the woods they came upon the chief's wife and children. From these, with the help of Melchor, an Indian interpreter who had traveled with Francisco Hernández and

Hernán Cortés disembarking on the island of Cuzmil, today Cozumel.

also Grijalva, they discovered that she was the chief's wife. Cortés presented her and her children with many gifts and had them send for the chief. When he arrived Cortés treated him very kindly, giving him some small gifts; he delivered his wife and children to him and returned all the things that had been taken in the town. He begged him to make the Indians return to their homes, and when they did, he returned to each one everything that was his. Having reassured them thus, he spoke to them on the emptiness of idols and urged them to adore the Cross; and this he set up in their temples together with a picture of Our Lady. With this he ended the people's idolatry.

Here Cortés heard that six days' march away there were bearded men in the power of a chief, and tried to persuade the Indians to seek them; he did find one to go, but it was difficult because they were afraid of the chief with the bearded men. He wrote this letter:

"Noble sirs: I left Cuba with eleven ships in my fleet and 500 Spaniards, and landed here on Cozumel, from where I write this letter. The people of this island have assured me that there are five or six bearded men in this country that resemble us in all aspects. They are unable to tell me more, but from this I reckon and feel certain that you are Spaniards. I and these gentlemen who are come with me to explore and settle these new lands do earnestly beg you to come to us within six

Maya shrine on Cuzmil.

days of receiving this message, without more delay or excuse. Do you come, we shall recognize and reward the good offices that this fleet shall receive from you. I send a brigantine for you to come in, and two ships for protection."

The Indians took this letter tied up in their hair and delivered it to Aguilar, but they were away longer than the period stated, so those on the ships thought they had been killed and returned to the port of Cozumel. Seeing that neither the Indians nor the bearded men arrived, Cortés set sail next day. However, that very day one of the ships sprang a leak and they were obliged to return to port. While the leak was being repaired Aguilar, who had received the letter, crossed the stretch of sea between Yucatán and Cozumel by canoe. When those of the fleet sighted him they went out to see who it was. Aguilar asked them if they were Christians, and when they replied that they were, and Spanish, Aguilar wept for joy, and falling to his knees gave thanks to God, then asked the Spaniards if it was Wednesday.

They took Aguilar, naked as he stood, to Cortés, who gave him clothing and treated him with great kindness. There, Aguilar told the story of the shipweck, his troubles and the death of his companions, and explained how it had been impossible to inform Guerrero in such a short time as he was more than eighty leagues away.

With the help of Aguilar, who was a very good interpreter, Cortés returned to preaching the worship of the Cross and removed idols from the temples. The preaching of Cortés is said to have made such a deep impression on the natives of Cozumel that they would go to the beach and chant to passing Spaniards *Marìa, Marìa; Cortés, Cortés.*

Cortès left, put in briefly at Campeche, but did not land until he reached Tabasco where, among the gifts and women offered to him was an Indian girl who was afterwards called Marina. She was from Xalisco, daughter of noble parents who had been stolen when small and sold in Tabasco. From there she had been sold again in Xicalango, then in Champotón, where she learned the language of Yucatán, in which she communicated with Aguilar. Thus, God provided Cortés with good and faithful interpreters, with whose help he came to acquire knowledge and familiarity in Mexican affairs for Marina knew a great deal from having been in contact with Indian merchants and high-ranking people who spoke about them every day.

V

Provinces of Yucatán.
The most important ancient buildings

Some old men in Yucatán say that they heard from their forefathers that this land was first settled by a certain people that came from the East whom God had delivered by opening twelve paths for them through the ocean. Be this true, all the inhabitants of the Indies must be descended from the Jews, because having once crossed the Straits of Magellan they must have spread gradually over the more than 2,000 leagues of territory that Spain now governs.

The tongue of this country is one and the same, and this was a great help in converting it, although on the coast there are some differences in words and manner of speech. Those on the coast are indeed more sophisticated in their behavior and language: the women cover their breasts, which further inland they do not do.

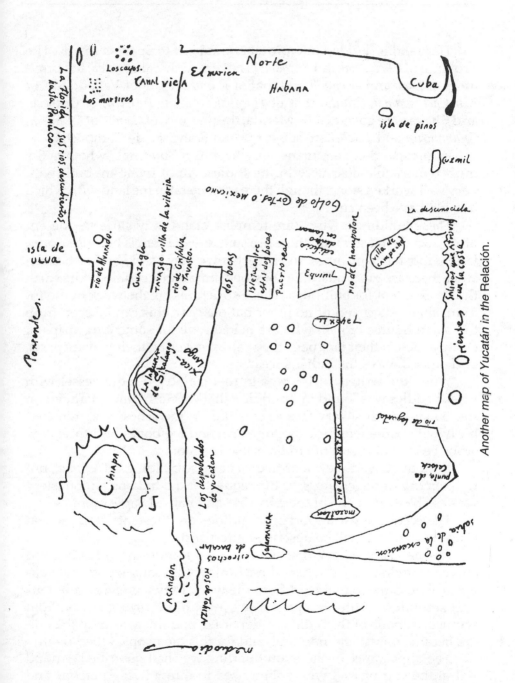

Another map of Yucatán in the Relación.

This land is divided into provinces, subject to Spanish towns. The province of *Chectemal* and *Bachalal* is governed by Salamanca; the provinces of *Ekab* and *Cochuah* and that of *Kupul* are under Valladolid; *An Kin Chel, Izamal, Zotuta,* that of *Hocabai Humun, Tutuxiú,* of *Cehpech,* and Chakan are governed by Merida; the province of *Camol,* of *Campech, Champutun* and *Tixchel* are subject to San Francisco de Campeche.

In Yucatán there are many very beautiful buildings, which is the most remarkable discovery in the Indies. All of them are built with very well worked stone, though there is no metal in the land with which it could have been cut.

These buildings, which are temples, stand very close to one another and the reason why there are so many of them is because populations moved many times, and in each town they would build a temple, since there are great quantities of stone, lime and a certain white earth that is excellent for buildings. These structures are the work of the Indians themselves and of no other nations, and this can be seen from the stone figures of men who are naked save for some long strips of cloth, which in their language they call *ex,* covering their private parts, and other devices the Indians wear.

When the writer, a friar, was in that country, a large vessel with three handles was found in a building that was torn down, painted on the outside with silvery flames, and inside the ashes of a cremated body with some wondrously large arm and leg bones and three fine stone beads of the sort the Indians used as money.

In all there were eleven or twelve of these buildings at *Yzamal,* but no memory of the creators; at the request of the Indians a monastery was established in one of them in 1549 and named San Antonio.

The second most important buildings are those at *Tikoch* and at *Chichenizá,* which will be described afterwards.

Chichenizá is a very fine site lying ten leagues from Izamal and eleven from Valladolid where three brothers are said to have ruled as lords, who came to that land from the west. They were very religious and so built beautiful temples. They lived most virtuously, without women, but one of them died or departed, and this was why the others became unjust and immoral, and for this the people killed them.

The appearance of the main building we shall describe later and tell of the sort of well where they used to throw living persons and precious objects in sacrifice. The well is more than seven times the height of a man down to the water and much more than one hundred feet

Representation of Kukulcán at Chichén Itzá.

across, a circle wonderfully cut out of the rock. The water seems to be green, which people say is because of the woods that surround it.

VI

Kukulkán. The founding of Mayapán

It is the belief of the Indians that with the *Ytzaes* who founded *Chichenizá* there ruled a great lord named *Cuculcán*, and the proof of this is the main building, which is called *Cuculcán*. They say that he arrived from the west, but disagree as to whether he came before or after the *Yzaes*, or with them. They say that he was well-favored and had neither wife nor children, and that on his return he was held in Mexico as one of their gods and called *Cezalcuati*. Also in Yucatán he was regarded as a god because he was a great statesman, and this was seen in the order

Maya priest.

he brought to Yucatán after the death of the rulers to calm the dissent that their deaths caused in the land.

The same Cuculcán turned to establishing another city, making an agreement with the native rulers of the land that both he and they should go there and that all affairs and business should be taken there. For this he chose a very fine site eight leagues farther inland from where Mérida now stands, and fifteen or sixteen leagues from the sea. There they enclosed about one eighth of a league with a very thick wall of dry stone, leaving only two narrow gateways in the low wall. Inside this enclosure they built their temples. The greatest, which is like the one at *Chichenizá*, they named Cuculcán. They built another, round, with four entrances, different from all the others there are in that land, and others surrounding it, close to one another. In this enclosed space they made houses for the rulers. Among these they only divided the land, giving villages to each one in accordance with the age of his lineage and his person. And Cuculcán named the city, not giving it his own as the *Ahizaes* did in *Chichenizá*, meaning "Well of the Aizaes", but calling it *Mayapán*, which is to say *"Pennon of Maya"* because the tongue of the land is called *Maya*. The Indians call the city *Ychpa*, which means "Within the Walls".

Cuculcán lived with the chiefs in this city for some years then, leaving them in firm peace and amity returned to Mexico along the same road. On the way he stayed briefly at Champotón where, in memory of himself and of his departure, he put up a fine building like the one at *Chichenizá* a long stone-throw away from the coast. And thus *Cuculcán* left a permanent memorial in Yucatán.

VII

Government, priesthood, science, letters and books in Yucatán

When *Cuculcán* left the chiefs agreed, for the republic to survive, that the house of the *Cocomes* should have supreme authority since it was the oldest and richest and the head at that time was a man of great worth. When this had been done, they then decreed that since there were only temples and houses for the lords and the high priest inside the enclosed area, houses should be built outside the walls where each of these might house his servants and where the people of his villages might lodge whenever they came to the city for reasons of trade. Each one put his steward in these houses; he carried a short, thick rod as a sign of his office and was called a *Caluac*. This steward kept account of the villages and of who governed them, and they also would advise about what was needed in the house of the ruler, such as birds, maize, honey, salt, fish, game, clothes and other items. The *Caluac* would always be present in the chief's house to see what was lacking there, and would provide it immediately, because the house was his master's storeroom.

Their custom was to seek out the invalids and the blind in the villages and provide for them. The chiefs appointed governors and, if these were faithful to them, passed on the office to their sons. They were charged to deal fairly with the common people, to keep the peace in the village and to ensure that all worked to support themselves and the rulers.

All the chieftains took care to respect, visit and please *Cocom*, accompanying him, feasting him and addressing themselves to him on difficult matters. And all lived together in harmony and with their accustomed amusements of dancing, feasts and hunting.

The people of Yucatán were as meticulous in religious matters as in government. They had a high priest called *Ah Kin May*, whose name was *Ahau Kin May*, meaning *High Priest May*, who was greatly revered by the chiefs. He had both Indians and offerings set apart for him, and in addition the chiefs presented him with gifts, and all the priests of the villages sent him contributions. His sons or his nearest relatives succeeded him in importance, and in this lay the key to their lore, for this was what they dealt with most. They gave the chiefs advice and answers to their questions, and seldom concerned themselves with sacrifices save at the major festivals or in matters of great importance. These men provided priests for the villages when they were needed, examining them in their lore and ceremonies; then they put them in charge of the duties of their office and of setting a good example to the village, and provided them with books. These also attended to the upkeep of the temples, taught their knowledge, and wrote books on it.

They taught the sons of the other priests and the second sons of the chiefs, who were taken to them as children for this if they were seen to be disposed towards this task.

The things that they taught were the reckoning of years, months and days, the festivals and the ceremonies, the administration of their sacraments the days and times of ill omen, their manners of divination, remedies for sickness and afflictions, ancient lore, and reading and writing with the letters and characters they used for writing, with figures that the writings referred to.

They used to write their books on a long sheet folded in pleats that was held closed between two boards that they would make very fine; they wrote on one side and on the other, in accordance with the folds. This paper they made from the roots of a tree and gave a white gloss that was good for writing on. Some important chiefs were versed in these matters out of curiosity, and thus were more highly regarded, but they did not practice them publicly.

Codex painter.

VIII

Arrival of the Tutul-Xiú and the alliance they made with the rulers of Mayapán. The tyranny of Cocom. The loss of his power and the fall of the city of Mayapán.

The Indians tell that many tribes and their chiefs came to Yucatán from the south. They seem to have come from Chiapas, but the Indians do not know this; rather the present writer surmises this because many words and verbal forms are the same in Chiapas as in Yucatán, and there are many signs in the region of Chiapas of places that have been abandoned. They say that these peoples wandered through the wilds of Yucatán for forty years where they had no water save that which fell

Lords of the Maya ruling class.

as rain; that at the end of this time they reached the lines of hills that lie almost opposite the city of *Mayapán*, ten leagues distant. There they began to settle and constructed splendid buildings in many places, and the people of *Mayapán* became most friendly towards them, being content to see that they cultivated the land as if natives of it. Thus, these *Tutu Xiú* placed themselves under the laws of *Mayapàn* and people of the two tribes married; and since the lord *Xiú* of the *Tutu-Xiú* was one of these he came to be highly respected by all.

These peoples lived so peacefully that there was no discord at all, and they used neither arms nor bows, not even for hunting, though they are excellent bowmen now. They used only snares and traps, with which they took game in plenty. The priests had a certain skill in throwing spears with the aid of a wooden bar some three fingers wide and six spans long with a groove hollowed for a third of the way along. With this and some cords they could throw strongly and accurately.

They had laws against wrongdoers and applied them strictly. such as against an adulterer, whom they delivered to the injured party for him either to execute by dropping a great stone on his head from on high, or for him to pardon if he so desired. For adultresses they had no punishment except the shame, which a very serious matter among them. He who ravished a maiden they would stone to death, and they tell of one case: that the chief of the *Tutu-Xiú* had a brother who was accused of this crime, and he had him stoned then covered with a great mound of stones. And they had a law before this city was established that ordered adulterers punished by haing their intestines drawn out through the navel.

The *Cocom* governor became covetous of wealth and for this reason talked with those of the garrison that the kings of Mexico kept in Tabasco and Xicalango, promising to deliver the city to them. Thus he brought the Mexica people to Mayapán, oppressed the poor, and enslaved many. The chiefs would have killed him, had they not been afraid of the Mexica. The lord of the *Tuluxiues* never consented to this, and when those of Yucatán saw themselves thus oppressed, they learned the use of arms from the Mexica and so acuired such mastery in the use of the bow and arrow, the spear and the ax, their shields and their strong tunics padded with cotton and other implements of war that they were no longer in awe of the Mexica nor feared them; rather they considered them of little account. Thus passed several years.

This *Cocom* was the first to make people slaves, and from this evil arose the use of weapons to defend themselves so that all would not become slaves.

Among the successors of the house of *Cocom* there was a very arrogant man who imitated *Cocom*, and he made another alliance with those of Tabasco, introduced more Mexica into the city and began to tyrannize and enslave the lower people. For this reason the chiefs joined the faction of *Tutu Xiú*, who was a great statesman like his ancestors and plotted to slay Cocom. And thus they did, also killing all his children except ome who was absent; they plundered his houses and took possession of all the land he had planted with cacao and other produce, claiming that with these all he had stolen from them would be repaid. The opposition between the *Cocomes* —who said they had been unjustly ousted— and the *Xiues* went on for so long that after having been more than 500 years in the city they deserted it and left it and left in unpeopled, with each going to his own land.

IX

Chronological monuments of Mayapán. Founding of the Zotuta reign. Origin of the Cheles. The three principal realms in Yucatán.

According to the count of the Indians, Mayapán was abandoned some 120 years ago; and there are in the main square of this city seven or eight stones ten feet tall, rounded on one side and well carved. On them are characters that they use, but so worn away by rain that they cannot be read; however the Indians believe that they record the foundation and the destruction of the city. There are other similar ones at *Zilán*, a town on the coast, though taller. And questioned as to what these were, the natives answered that it was their custom to set up one of these stones every 20 years, which is the number they use to count time. Yet this explanation does not seem to hold true, because in accordance with it there would be many more, and also because there are none in other towns save *Mayapán* and *Zilán*.

The principal thing that these chiefs who despoiled *Mayapán* took off to their own lands were the books of knowledge because they were always most obedient to the words of their priests, this being the reason there are so many temples in those provinces.

The son of *Cocom*, who had escaped death by being away engaged in commerce in the lands of *Ulúa*, which lie beyond the city of Salamanca, on learning of his father's death and the destruction of the city, returned forthwith. Gathering together his relatives and vassals he established a place that he named *Tibulón*, which means "we were betrayed". And they built many other towns in those forests, where many families of these *Cocomes* came together. The province where this chief rules is called *Zututa*.

The rulers of *Mayapán* did not take vengeance on the Mexica who assisted *Cocom* because they had been swayed by the governor of the province and because they were outlanders. So they let them be, allowing them to choose either to found a town for themselves apart or to leave the country, being as they were forbidden to marry local women but only among themselves. They elected to remain in Yucatán and not to return to the lagoons and mosquitoes of Tabasco and settled in the province of *Canul*, which was assigned to them. There they remained until the second attack by the Spanish.

It is said that among the twelve priests of Mayapán there was one most wise who had but one daughter, whom he married to a young noble named *Ah Chel*. Their sons were named like their father, after the custom of this land. People say that this priest advised his son-in-law of the destruction of the city and that the young man learned much from his father-in-law who, it is said, wrote certain characters on the flat of his left arm that were very powerful in ensuring respect. So favored, he established settlements on the coast until he finally founded *Tikoch*, with great numbers of people following him. This community of the *Chel* family was most distinguished and they peopled the most famous province of Yucatán, which they called, because of their name, the province of *Ah Kin Chel*. Here is *Ytzamal*, where the *Chel* resided, and they multiplied in Yucatán until governor Montejo arrived.

Among the three noble houses, which were the *Cocom*, the *Xiú* and the *Chel* there was great feud and enmity, and there still is today, even though they are now Christians. The *Cocom* said to the *Xiú* that they were intruders and also traitors because they had killed their chief and stolen his property. The *Xiú* said they were as the *Cocom*, just as ancient and noble and that they were not traitors but liberators of the country since they had slain a tyrant. The *Chel* ruler said that he was equal to them in lineage, being the grandson of a priest, the most respected one of *Mayapán*, and that in himself he was better than they were as he had known how to make himself as much a lord as them. They were even unpleasant to each other in the matter of food, for the *Chel*, who were on the coast, refused to give either fish or salt to the *Cocom*, obliging them to travel a great distance to obtain these things; and the *Cocom* would not allow the *Chel* either to hunt or take fruit.

X

Several disasters suffered in Yucatán in the century before the Conquest: hurricanes, plagues, wars, etc.

These people enjoyed more than twenty years of plenty and good health, and multiplied so greatly that the whole country appeared to be one town. It was at this time that they built the temples in such large numbers as can be seen today in all quarters; and going through the forests one can see the remains of houses and finely constructed buildings among the trees.

After this time of prosperity, one winter evening at about six o'clock a wind arose that steadily grew into a raging hurricane. The wind blew down all the large trees, slaughtering all kinds of animals in large numbers, and it brought down the tall houses which, since they were of wattle and had fires inside because of the cold, caught fire and burned most of the people to death; and if any ran away they were killed by blows from falling wood. The hurricane lasted until noon the next day, when it was seen that those living in small houses had escaped harm, among them being the newly married couples who there used to build small huts opposite the house of their parents or parents-in-law where they lived for the first years. And thus, the land lost the name "Land of Deer and Turkeys" that it used to be called and was left so treeless that those there are now seem to have been planted all together so equally grown are they. Looking at the country from high ground, it appears to have been clipped with shears.

Those who survived took heart, building and cultivating the land, and multiplied greatly in sixteen years of health and good seasons. The last one was the most fertile of all, but when they were ready to begin harvesting the crops there came to the whole country pestilential fevers that lasted twenty-four hours; and when the fever was gone, those infected swelled up and burst open full of maggots. Many people died of this pestilence and most of the crops were left unharvested.

When this plague was over they enjoyed another sixteen good years, during which their animosities and feuds were revived so that 150,000 men died in battles. With this slaughter they became quiet and made peace, and lived at ease for twenty years. After this time they were struck by a plague of boils that rotted their bodies with a foul stench so that their limbs dropped off in pieces in three or four days.

It must be more than fifty years since this last plague occurred, and the slaughter of the war was twenty years earlier, and the plague of the swelling and maggots was sixteen years before the wars, and the hurricane another sixteen before this, twenty-two or twenty-three years after the destruction of the city of *Mayapán*. So, according to this reckoning the city was destroyed 125 years ago, years during which the people of this country have suffered the great misfortunes described and many others that began when the Spanish started to arrive, both through wars and other punishments that God sends, so that it is a marvel that there are any people at all, few though they are.

XI

Prophecies about the arrival of the Spanish. Biography of Francisco de Montejo, first governor general of Yucatán.

Just as the Mexica had signs and prophecies about te coming of the Spanish and the end of their power and religion, so did the people of Yucatán have them some years before the governor general Montejo conquered them. In the hills of *Maní*, which is in the province of *Tutu-Xiú*, an Indian named *Ah Cambal*, whose office was that of *Chilám*, who is the one charged with giving the replies of the heathen god, told them publicly that they would soon be ruled by foreign people who would preach to them of a God and the virtue of a wooden post which in their language they call *Vamonché*, meaning 'upright post with great power against demons'.

The next in line of the *Cocom*, called Don Juan Cocom after being baptized, was a man of great reputation, very learned in many things, and very sagacious and with a good understanding of the Indians. He was on very friendly terms with te author of this book, Friar Diego de

*Francisco de Montejo, the conqueror and first governor
of governor of Yucatán.*

Landa, and related to him many things about ancient times, and showed
him a book that had been his grandfather's, son of the *Cocom* who was
killed at *Mayapán*, in which a deer was painted. His grandfather had
told him that when large deer (for thus they called cows) should enter
that country, the worship of the gods would come to and end; and this
had come about, because the Spanish brought large cows.

The governor, Francisco de Montejo, was a native of Salamanca,
and came to the Indies after the city of Santo Domingo and the island
of Hispaniola had ben settled, having first lived in Seville for a time,
where he left an infant son he had there. He came to the city on the
island of Cuba, where he earned a living and made many friends because of his fine character. Among them was Diego Velázquez, the governor of the island, and Hernando Cortés. As the governor decided to
send Juan de Grijalva, his nephew, to trade in the lands of Yucatán and
to discover new land after the news that Francisco Hernández de
Córdoba brought when he discovered it, saying that it was a rich land,
he decided that Montejo should go with him. Since Montejo was
wealthy he provided one of the ships and many supplies and so was

one of the second Spanish party to reach Yucatán. Once he had seen the coast of Yucatán he wished to make himself rich there rather than in Cuba.

When he learned of Cortés' decision, he put himself and his wealth at his disposal, and Cortés gave him a ship to command, making him captain of it. In Yucatán they were joined by Gerónimo de Aguilar, from whom Montejo learned the language of that country and about its affairs. Reaching New Spain, Cortés began to found settlements, and the first town he named Vera Cruz, after the escutcheon on his flag. In this town Montejo was appointed King's Magistrate, a post he held with discretion, and was publicly named as such by Cortés when he returned from a voyage he made around the coast. For this reason Cortés sent him to Spain as one of the representatives of New Spain and to take to the king the royal fifth in taxes with an account of the land discovered and of the things that were beginning to be done there.

When Francisco de Montejo reached the Court of Castile, the president of the Council of the Indies was Juan Rodríguez de Fonseca, Bishop of Burgos. He had false information against Cortés from Diego de Velásquez, the governor of Cuba, who aspired to be governor of New Spain also. Most members of the Council were hostile to the doings of Cortés, saying that it seemed he was not sending money to the King but rather asking him for it; that he knew that the Emperor was in Flanders and for this reason was acquitting himself ill. Montejo persevered for seven years, from when he left the Indies in 1519 until he embarked, which was in 1526. Such was his perseverance that he callenged the authority of the president and of Pope Adrian, who was regent, and spoke with the Emperor himself, which proved of great benefit, as the business of Cortés was settled as was fit.

XII

Montejo sails to Yucatán and takes possession of the country. The Chels yield to thim the town of Chichén Itzá. The Indians oblige him to leave them.

At the time Montejo was at Court he secured for himself the commission to conquer Yucatán, although he could have bargained for other things, and was given the title of Governor and Captain General. He next went to Seville, taking with him a nephew thirteen years old who had the same name as his own, and in Seville found his son, now twenty-eight years old, whom he took with him. He arranged a marriage with a lady of Seville, a rich widow, and thus was able to muster 500 men, whom he embarked on three ships. He set out on his voyage and landed at *Cuzmil*, an island of Yucatán, where the Indians did not defy him because they had been made gentle by the Spanish followers of Cortés. There he was able to learn many words from the Indians to communicate with them. From here he sailed to Yucatán and took possession of it, with one of his standard-bearers, banner in hand, saying: "In the name of God I take possession of this land for God and for the King of Castile."

Then he sailed fown the coast, which well settled, until he came to *Conil*, a town on that same coast. The Indians became alarmed to see so many horses and men, and warned all the people of what was happening, waiting to see what the intention of the Spanish was.

The Indian rulers of the province of *Chicaca* came to visit the Governor as a sign of peace and were welcomed. Among them there was a very strong man who seized a cutlass from a young negro bearing it behind his master and tried to kill the Governor with it. He defended himself until the other Spaniards reached him; they thus understood that it was necessary to proceed with caution.

Montejo made inquiries as to which was the largest town and learned that it was *Tekoch*, where the *Chel* ruled, which lay further down the coast on the course the Spanish were following. The Indians, believing that they were on their way out of the country, did not grow hostile or hinder them on their journey. Thus they reached *Tekoch*, which they found to be a larger and finer town than they had thought. The Governor was pleased that the rulers of that country were not the *Couohes* of Champotón, who were always more spirited than the *Chel* who, with the priesthood that still exists today, are not as arrogant as others. For this reason, they granted the Governor leave to make a town for his followers, and for this gave them *Chichenizá*, an excellent site seven leagues away. From here he gradually conquered the country, which he did easily because the *Ah Kin Chel* people did not resist him, and those of *Tutu Xiú* aided him; because of this, the others put up little opposition.

Thus, the Governor asked for men to build at *Chichenizá* and in a short time raised a town, making the houses of wood and the roofs of leaves from a certain palm and long grass in the manner of the Indians. He saw that the Indians served without any ill-will. He counted the people of the country, who were many, and divided the towns among the Spanish, and they say that even the man with the smallest allotment received two or three thousand Indians. Thus he began to give orders to the natives on how they had to serve that city, which did not much please the Indians, but they concealed this for the moment.

XIII

Montejo leaves Yucatán with his men and goes to Mexico. His son, Francisco de Montejo, afterwards pacifies the land.

Montejo did not build defenses in the settlement against enemies because it was too far from the sea to give access to and from the City of Mexico and for goods from Spain. It appeared a humiliation to the Indians that they had to serve foreigners where they were rulers, and they began to attack on all sides. Although Montejo defended himself with his horses and men, and killed many of them, the Indians were reinforced every day and so the food supplies ran out. At last they left the city one night, leaving a dog on a leash tied to the clapper of a bell with a piece of bread placed out of reach. That same day they exhausted the Indians with skirmishes so that they would not follow them. The dog would ring the bell as it tried to reach the bread, and this made the Indians wonder if they were about to come out and attack. On discovering this they felt humiliated by the trick and decided to hunt for the Spanish in all directions because they did not know what route they were taking. The men who went by the same road caught up with the Spanish, making a great hue and cry as if against fugitives. So, six men on horseback waited for them in open country and killed many of them with their lances. One of the Indians seized a horse by its leg and brought it down as if it had been a sheep. The Spanish reached *Zilán*, which was a very lovely town whose ruler was a young *Chel*, a Christian and friendly towards the Spanish, who treated them well. *Zilán* was very close to *Tikoch* that, with all the other towns on that coast, was ruled by the *Chel*. Thus they allowed them to live in safety for some months.

The Governor, realizing that from there they would not be able to receive assistance from New Spain and that if the Indians attacked them they would be lost, decided to move on to Campeche and from there to the City of Mexico, leaving Yucatán without forces. It was forty-eight leagues from *Zilán* to Campeche through well populated country. They told *Vamux Chel*, the ruler of *Zilán*, of their plans and he offered to ensure the road was safe for them and to go with them. Montejo talked with the chief's uncle, who was ruler of Yobain, and arranged for him to give him two fine-looking sons he had to accompany him. And so, with the three young cousins, two riding together and the chief of *Zilán* mounted on a horse alone, they reached Campeche safely, where they were welcomed. The *Chels* took their leave but on the way to their towns the one from *Zilán* died. From there they set out for the City of Mexico, where Cortés had set aside an allotment of Indians for Montejo even though he had been absent.

Very soon after the Governor had arrived in the City of Mexico with his son and his nephew, his wife, Doña Beatriz de Herrera arrived in search of him with a daughter he had by her called Catalina de Montejo. The Governor had married Beatriz de Herrera secretly in Seville, and some say that he repudiated her, but Don Antonio de Mendoza, the Viceroy of New Spain, intervened and thus he recognized her. The same Viceroy sent him as governor to Honduras, where he married his daughter to lawyer Alonso Maldonado, President of the Audiencia of the Border Areas. Some years later he was moved to Chiapas from where he sent his son to Yucatán, with full powers, and he conquered and pacified it.

Don Francisco, the Governor's son, grew up at the court of Ferdinand V, the Catholic King, and his father brought him to the Indies when he returned to conquer Yucatán; and from there he accompanied him to Mexico. The viceroy Don Antonio and the marquis Don Hernán Cortés found him personable, and he went with the marquis on the journey to California. On his return the viceroy named him governor of Tabasco and he married a lady by the name of Andrea del Castillo who had arrived in Mexico as a young girl in the company of relatives.

XIV

The position of Yucatán after the departure of the Spanish. Don Francisco, the governor's son, reestablishes Spanish rule in Yucatán.

When the Spanish departed from Yucatán there was drought in the land, and because maize had been used without regard during the wars against the Spanish, a famine ensued. It was so grave that they even ate the bark of trees, especially of one they call *cumché*, which is spongy and soft inside. Because of this famine the *Xiú*, who rule *Maní* determined to make a solemn sacrifice to the idols, taking some male and female slaves to throw into the well of Chichenizá. However, as they had to pass by the town of the *Cocom* chiefs, their sworn enemies, and reasoning that old quarrels would be renewed, they sent to beg to be allowed to pass through their territory. The *Cocom* deceived them by sending a favorable answer but, giving them lodging all together in a large hut, they set fire to it and slew those who ran away. Because of this episode there were great wars. In addition, locusts increased throughout five years and left them no greenery. And they suffered so

Battle between Maya warriors and Spaniards.

much hunger that they would fall dead at the roadside. It was such that when the Spanish returned they did not recognize the land although after four good years since the plague of locusts it was somewhat recovered.

Don Francisco de Montejo left for Yucatán following the rivers of Tabasco and entered the region through the lagoons of Dos Bocas. The first place he called at was Champotón whose ruler *Moch Covoh* had caused so much trouble for Francisco Hernández and Grijalva. But he was now dead, so there was no resistance shown there, rather the townspeople supported Don Francisco and his men for two years, the time in which he could not go forward because of the great opposition he met. Afterwards he went to Campeche and came to form great friendship with the people of this town. Thus, with their assitance and that of Campotón he concluded the conquest, promising that they would be rewarded by the King for their loyalty, although the King has not yet kept this promise.

Resistance was not enought to prevent Don Francisco and his army from reaching Tihó, where he founded the city of Mérida. Leaving their pack animals in Mérida, they proceeded with the conquest, sending captains in various directions. Don Francisco sent his cousin Francisco de Montejo to the town of Valladolid to pacify the tribes, which were somewhat rebellious and to establish the city as it is now. In *Chectemal* he founded the town of Salamanca, and had already settled Campeche. Then he gave orders about the duties of the Indians and the goverment by the Spanish until his father arrived from Chiapas with his wife and household to govern. He was welcomed in Campeche, calling the town San Francisco because of his own name, and then continued to the city of Mérida.

XV

The cruelty of the Spanish to the natives. How they excused themselves.

The Indians accepted the yoke of servitude reluctantly. Though the Spanish kept the towns all over the country properly allotted, there was sure to be someone among the Indians who would stir them to hostility. Very cruel punishnents were administered because of this, which was the reason why the population diminished. They burned alive several of the leading men of the province of Cupul, and hanged others. Accusations were made against the people of Yobain, a *Chel* town; the leading men were taken and, in shackles, put into a house to which they then set fire, burning them alive with the greatest inhumanity that can be imagined. And I, Diego de Landa, can say that I saw a great tree near the town on which a captain hanged many Indian women from the branches and hung their small children from their feet. In this same town and in another called Verey, two leagues away, they hanged two Indian women, one a virgin and the other newly married, not because they were guilty of anything but because they were very beautiful and the Spanish feared that the troops might molest them, and also to show the Indians that their women were of no importance to them. The memory of these two still lives among both Indians and Spanish because of their great beauty and the heartlessness with which they were killed.

The Indians of the *Cochua* and *Chectemal* provinces revolted and the Spanish suppressed them in such a manner that these two provinces, originally the most settled and populous, were left the most wretched in the whole of that country. They inflicted outrageous cruelty on the Indians, cutting off their noses, arms and legs; they cut the breasts off the women and threw them into deep lagoons with gourds tied to their feet; they wounded children with spearthrusts because they could not walk as fast as their mothers, and if they were chained together with collars and they fell sick or could not keep pace with the others, they cut off their heads instead of stopping to free them. They kept large numbers of men and women prisoner to serve them, treating them in the same way. It is said that Francisco de Montejo did not carry out any of these cruel acts, nor did he condone them; rather he disagreed with them completely, but was unable to do anything.

The Spanish excused themselves by saying that as they were so few, they could not keep so many people under control except by marking them afraid of terrible punishments, giving the example of the historic journey of the Hebrews to the promised land, when great cruelty was committed at God's command. On the other hand, the Indians were right to defend their liberty and to place their trust in the valiant leaders they had among them, believing that they would be so against the Spanish.

They tell the story of a Spanish crossbowman and an Indian archer, both very skillful, who were trying to kill each other, but they could not take each other off guard. The Spaniard pretended to drop his guard, putting one knee on the ground and the Indian shot an arrow into his hand that went up his arm, separating the bones from each other. But at the same time, the Spaniard loosed his crossbow and shot the Indian in the chest. The Indian, realizing that he was fatally wounded, cut a liana, which is like an osier but much longer, and hanged himself with it in the sight of all so that they would not say that a Spaniard had killed him. There are many instances of such courage.

XVI

The state of the country before the Conquest. An uprising. A royal decree in favor of the Indians. Death of Governor Montejo. His descendants.

Before the Spanish won that land the natives lived together in towns, with many many regulations, and they kept the land very clean and free of weeds and planted with fine trees. The arrangement was thus: in the center of the town were the houses of the chiefs and the priests, and the the most important people. Thus, the wealthiest and most repected lived near these houses, and on the edges of the town were the temples with fine squares, and all around the temples were the houses of the common people. The wells, if there were few, were near the houses of the chiefs. Their farmlands were planted with wine-rees and they grew cotton, peppers and maize. They lived in these communities out of fear of their enemies, who used to take them prisoner, but because of the wars with the Spanish they disappeared into the forests.

The Indians of Valladolid, either because of their evil nature or because of the ill-treatment of the Spanish, plotted to kill them when they separated to collect their tribute. In one day they killed seventeen Spaniards and 400 servants of the dead and those who were left alive. Then they sent arms and feet all over the land as a sign of what they had done so that others would rise up. But they would not do this, and so the Governor was able to assist the Spanish of Valladolid and punish the Indians.

The Governor had trouble with the Spanish of Mérida, and all the greater with the Emperor's decree taking the Indians away from all the governors. An agent went to Yucatán and took the Governor's Indians away from him, placing them under the protection of the King. After this, the Royal Audiencia of the City of Mexico charged him with wrongdoing and transferred him to the Royal Council of the Indies in Spain where he died, burdened by the years and his labors. He left in Yucatán his wife Doña Beatriz, still richer now he had died; his son,

Don Francisco de Montejo, married in Yucatán; his daughter, Doña Catalina, married to the lawyer Alonso Maldonado, President of the Audiencias of Honduras and of Santo Domingo on the island of Hispaniola, and Don Juan Montejo, a Spaniard, and Don Diego, a mestizo son he had by an Indian woman.

Don Fransicso, after leaving government to his father, lived in his house as a private citizen as regards politics, though he was highly respected by all for having conquered, apportioned and governed that country. He went to Guatemala with his position of resident, then returned home. The children he had were Don Juan de Montejo, whom he married to Doña Isabel, from Salamanca; Doña Beatriz de Montejo, married to her uncle, a first cousin of her father's; and Doña Francisca de Montejo, who married Don Carlos de Arellano from Guadalajara. He died from a long sickness after having seen all his children married.

XVII

Arrival of the Spanish Franciscan friars in Yucatán. The protection they gave to the natives. Their troubles with the encomenderos.

Friar Jacobo de Testera, a Franciscan, arrived in Yucatàn and began teaching the sons of the Indians, but the Spanish soldiers wanted to employ the boys so much that they had no time left for learning the catechism. In addition, they became angry with the friars when they reprehended them for the wrongs they did to the Indians, and so friar Jacobo returned to Mexico, where he died. Later, firar Toribio Motolinia sent friars from Guatemala, and from Mexico friar Martín de Hojacastro sent more, who all settled at Campeche and Mérida, with the consent of the Governor and his son Don Francisco. These friars built a monastery at Mérida, as has been told, and set about learning the language, which was a difficult task.

The one who learned most was friar Luis de Villalpando, who began studying it with the help of signs and small stones. He reduced it to some manner of grammatical system and wrote a Christian catechism in the language, although there was much resistance from the Spanish, who were absolute masters and wanted everything that was done to be in furtherance of gain and tributes, and also from the Indians, who were trying to persist in their idalatrous behaviour and drunken dissipation. The task was hard mainly because they were so scattered through the forest.

The Spanish resented the friars building monasteries and drove away the children of the Indians on their estates so that they would not come to catechism. And two times they set fire to the monastery at Valladolid with its church, which was built of wood and dry grass. There was so much trouble that the friars were obliged to go and live among the Indians. And when the Indians of that province rose in protest, writing to the viceroy, Antonio de Mendoza, that they had rebelled because of their love for the friars, the viceroy ordered an investigation and discovered that at the time they rebelled the friars were not yet in that province. The Spanish colonists watched the friars by night, to the scandal of the Indians, investigated their ways, and withheld alms.

Seeing this danger, the friars sent one of their number to see the distinguished judge Cerrato, the Chief Magistrate of Guatemala and report to him about what was happening. After hearing about the disorderliness and unchristian ways of the Spanish, who took tribute completely at will, and as much as they could without orders from the King, and forced the Indians to give personal service in all kinds of work, even hiring them to carry loads, the judge established a scale of taxation that was very long, but tolerable. In it he specified what belonged to the Indian after payment of tribute to his master, and that not everything belonged absolutely to the Spanish.

The estate owners appealed against this and, out of fear of the tax list, took even more from the Indians than until then. Therefore, the friars turned once more to the Audiencia and made petitions in Spain, doing so much that the Audiencia of Guatemala sent a Magistrate. He established a tax on land and abolished personal service; he obliged some of the colonists to marry, shutting the houses they had full of women. This man was the lawyer Tomás López, a native of Tendilla, and what he did made the colonists hate the friars even more, so that they spread libellous rumours about them and stopped attending their masses.

This hatred caused the Indians to behave very well towards the friars in consideration of the trouble they took without thought of gain to give them their freedom. So much that they did nothing without first informing the friars and taking their advice. This caused the Spanish to say out of bitterness that the friars had done all this to govern the Indies themselves and enjoy all the things that had been taken from them.

XVIII

The vices of the Indians. The friars study the language of the country. Their teachings to the natives. The punishments for apostates.

The vices of the Indians were idolatry, repudiation of their wives, public gluttony, and buying and selling slaves; and because the friars kept them from these things, they began to hate them. However, apart from the Spanish, those who harassed the friars most, though in secret, were the priests, being people who had lost their position and its benefits.

The way used for teaching the Indian was to collect together the small children of the rulers and most important families and settle them around the monasteries in houses that each town would build for its own people. Thus, all the children from each place were together, and their parents and relatives brought them food. And, together with these children they introduced those who came to Christain teaching, and as a result of such frequent visits many devoutly asked to be baptized. These children, after being taught, dutifully informed the friars of idolatrous practices and licentiousness, and would break idols, even if they belonged to their parents. They exhorted women who had been repudiated and orphans, if they were made slaves (either by the colonists or by the Indians themselves, the said), to complain to the friars. And although they were threatened by their own people, they did not stop; rather they replied that they were doing them an honor since it was for the good of their souls. Governor Montejo and the King's troops have always given the friars assistants to oblige the Indians to attend cat-

Converting the Indians.

echism and to punish those who went back to their old ways. At first the rulers were unwilling to hand over their children, thinking that the friars wanted to make them slaves, as the Spanish had done, and so sent many young slaves instead of their children, but when they understood the arrangement they gave them over readily. In this way, both the young made progress in the schools and the others in the catechism, which was admirable.

They learned how to read and write in the language of the Indians, which had been so reduced to a grammatical system that it was studied in the same way as Latin. It was found that they did not use six of our letters, namely D, F, G, Q, R and S, which they do not need at all. However, they needed to double some letters and add others to understand the many meanings of some words, because *Pa* means 'to open' and *PPa*, spoken with the lips pressed together tightly, means 'to break'; Tan is 'lime' or 'ash', and *Than*, said with force between the tongue and upper teeth means 'word' or 'to speak', and so with other words. Since they had different characters for these things it was not necessary to invent new symbols, but simply to put Latin letters to good use so that they would serve everyone.

They were also ordered to leave the houses they had in the forests and to settle together like earlier in proper villages so that they could be taught more easily and the friars would not have so many difficulties. They gave alms at Christmas and other festivals for the support of the friars, and also gave alms to the churches through two old Indians appointed for this purpose. With all this they gave the friars what was necessary when they went around visiting them and also furnished the churches with ornaments.

When the people were already instructed in religion and the young had made good progress, as we have said, they were perverted by the priests, who persisted in their idolatry, and by the chiefs and went back to worshiping idols and making sacrifices, not merely of incense but of human blood. The friars set up a court of inquiry about the matter, asking the magistrate for help, and many Indians were arrested and put on trial. An auto da fé was held, when many were put on scaffolds, with conical hats showing the crimes. Many Indians were whipped and their hair shorn, and some were made to wear a sanbenito for a time. Others, deluded by the devil, hanged themselves out of misery, but in general all showed great repentance and the willingness to be good Christians.

XIX

The arrival of Bishop Toral. Release of arbitrarily imprisoned Indians. Landa's voyage to Spain to justify the acts of the Franciscans.

At this point Francisco Toral, a Fransican friar originally from Ubeda who had been busy in Mexico for twenty years and was now coming as bishop of Yucatán arrived in Cámpeche. He, because of reports about the Spanish and the complaints of the Indians, countered all the friars had done and ordered the prisoners set free. The provincial was offended by this and he determined to go to Spain, first lodging a complaint in Mexico. Thus, he reached Madrid, where the members of the Council of the Indies severely reprimanded him for having overstepped his position as Bishop by assuming the powers of Inquisitor. In defense of this he pleaded the powers that his order had in the land, granted by Pope Adrian at the request of the Emperor and the assistance that the Royal Audiencia of the Indies had ordered to be given to him as a bishop. The council members were angered even further by these defenses and decided to refer him, with his own documents and those the bishop had sent against the friars to brother Pedro Bobadilla, Provincial of Castile. The king wrote to him, ordering him to examine the papers and give his judgment. Friar Pedro, since he was sick, entrusted the case to friar Pedro de Guzmán, who belonged to his own order, a learned man and expert in inquisitional affairs.

The opinions of seven learned men from Toledo were submitted: these were brother Francisco de Medina and brother Francisco Dorantes, belonging to the Franciscan order; teaching brother Alonso de la Cruz, an Augustine firar who had been thirty years in the Indies; the Lawyer Tomás López, who was Magistrate in the New Kingdom of Guatemala and judge in Yucatán; Hurtado, a professor of canon law; Mendez, professor of the Holy Scriptures, and Martínez, Scotist professor at Alcalá. These all declared that the provincial had been right in holding the auto da fé and in doing other things to castigate the Indians. Having seen this, brother Francisco de Guzmán wrote about it at length to the provincial, brother Pedro de Bobadilla.

The Indians of Yucatán merit the King's consideration for many things and for the willingness they have shown to serve him. When he was in need in Flanders his sister Princess Juana, who was regent sent a letter to those of the Indies to ask for aid. A magistrate of Guatemala carried this to Yucatán and then gathered together the rulers and ordered a friar to talk to them about what they owed to his majesty and what he was therefore asking of them. When the speech was over, two Indians rose to their feet and replied that they well knew they had an obligation towards God for having given them such a noble and most Christian king and that they regretted not living where they could serve him inperson; therefore, he should see what he wanted from them in their poverty and they would serve him with this, and if it were not enough they would sell their children and wives.

XX

The fashion of building houses in Yucatán. The obedience and respect of the Indians for their rulers. Their way of adorning their heads and wearing their clothes.

The fashion they had of building their houses was to cover them with thatch, which is very good and plentiful, or with the leaves of a special palm. They have very steep slopes so that they do no leak. Then they build a wall down the center that divides the house. In this wall they leave some openings into the half that they call the back of the house, where they have their beds. The other half they paint white with fine lime and the chiefs have this part painted with with many elegant designs also. This half is for receiving and lodging guests and has no doorway but is open for the whole length of the house. The eaves are very low in the front against the sun and rain and also, they say, for them to defend themselves against enemies out of the inner part when it is necessary.

Maya dwelling house

Inside a Maya hut.

The common people build the houses of the chiefs at their own expense. Since there are no doors it was considered a crime to do any wrong to the houses of other people. They had a small doorway at the back for necessary services and beds made of thin sticks with a mat on top where they sleep covered with their cotton cloaks. In summer they usually sleep on mats in the whitewashed part of the house, especially the men. In addition to building houses for the chiefs all the village people sowed their crops, cultivated them for them and harvested what was enough for him and his household. And when they went hunting or fishing, or it was the time to fetch salt, they always gave a part to the chief because they always did these things as a community.

If the chief died his eldest son would succeed him but the others were always greatly respected assisted and regarded as chiefs. They also helped important men of lower rank than the chief in all these things, in accordance with who they were or with the favor the chief showed them. The priests lived by means of their office and from offerings.

The chiefs ruled the village, settling disputes, ordering and arranging the affairs of their domains, all of which they did with the help of the leading men. They were carefully obeyed and highly respected, especially by the wealthy people they visited. They held court in their houses, where they settled cases and business matters, principally at night. If the chiefs left the village they took a large retinue, and it was the same when they left their houses.

The Indian men of Yucatán are fine-looking tall, well-built and very strong, and usually bow-legged because in their infancy, when their mothers carry them about they sit astride their hips. They considered it elegant to be cross-eyed, which their mothers induced artificially when they were infants by suspending a little ball of something from their hair that hung between their eyebrows. As it moved about, they would lift their eyes to it and finally become cross-eyed. The back of their head and forehead were flat, which was also something done deliberately by their mothers when they were children. Their ears were pierced for ornaments and much mutilated as a result of sacrifices. Their beard did not grow, and they said that their mothers would scorch their faces with hot cloths when they were young boys so that it would never appear. Nowadays they do have beard, but very coarse, like horsehair.

They wore their hair like the women: on top they singed a good-sized area, and thus the hair on the lower part of the head grew long and that on the crown was kept short. They braided it and made a

Costume.

wreath of it round their head, leaving the end behind like a tassel. All the men used mirrors, but not so the women, and to call any man a cuckold they used to say that his wife had put the mirror in the hair left at the back of his head. They bathed a lot, not troubling to cover themselves fom the women, save what could he covered by the hand. They were very fond of fragrance and therefore carried nosegays of sweet-smelling flowers and herbs carefully and skillfully made. It was their custom to paint their faces and bodies red, which did not become them at all, but they held it to be very elegant.

Their clothing was a strip of cloth one hand wide that served as both drawers and breeches that they wrapped around the waist several time in such a fashion that one of the ends hung in front and the other behind. These ends were made painstakingly by their wives, using featherwork. They wore long, square cloaks that they knotted on one shoulder, sandals of hemp or of untanned, dry deerskin, and no other garment.

XXI

The food and drink of the Indians of Yucatán.

Their staple food is maize, from which they make different dishes and drinks, and even when it is drunk the way they do, it serves as both food and drink. The Indian women put the maize to soak in lime and water the previous night, and in the morning it is soft and half-cooked, and in this state the skin and tip are removed. They then grind it on stones and give large balls and loads of this half-ground grain to laborers, traverlers and sailors; it keeps for several months, only becoming sour. They will take a lump of this and thin it with water in a vessel that is the rind of a fruit borne on a tree by which means God provided them with vessels. They drink this preparation and eat the rest, which is tasty and very nourishing. From the more finely ground maize they obtain milk and boil it down over the fire to make a sort of gruel that they drink hot in the mornings. On what remains from the morning they pour water for drinking through the day, because they do not drink plain water. They also toast the maize, grind it and mix it with water, adding to it a little chili pepper and cacao to make a very refreshing drink.

They make a delicious foaming drink out of maize and ground cacao with which they celebrate their festivals. They obtain a fat that is like butter from cacao and with this and maize prepare another delicious and much appreciated drink. Yet another drink they make from the raw paste of ground maize that is very refreshing and flavorful.

They make many kinds of bread that is both good and wholesome, except that it is bad eating when cold so the Indian women busy themselves making it twice a day. No way has been found to make flour that can be kneaded like wheat flour, and if ever anything is made in the style of wheat bread it is worthless.

They make dishes of vetables and of the flesh of deer, wild and domestic birds, of which there are many, and of fish, which are plentiful. Thus they have good rations, especially since they have begun to raise pigs and birds come from Spain.

In the mornings the take the hot drink with chili, as we have remarked, and during the day the other cold drinks, and at night they have the cooked dishes. If there is no meat they make their stews of peppers and vegetables. It was not the custom for the women to eat with the men. The men would eat separately from the floor or at most with a mat serving as a table. They eat well when they have the means, and when not, endure hunger very well and satisfy themselves with very little. They wash their hands and mouths after eating.

XXII

The Indians' painting and tattooing. Their drunkenness, feasts, pantomimes, music and dances.

They used to tattoo their bodies, and the more they did so the stronger and more valiant they were held to be because tattooing was a most painful process. It was thus: the tattooer first colored in the design where

Musicians.

it was wanted then made delicate incisions on the painting and thus, with the mixture of blood and pigment the picture remained on the body. Tattooing was done little by little because of te great pain it caused. After it people fell sick because the tattooed places became inflamed and suppurated, yet they ridiculed those who did not have themselves tattooed.

They flatter themselves on being refined and possessing natural good manners and graces and on now eating and drinking as we do.

The Indians were very dissolute, drinking until they were intoxicated, from which many evils arose such as killing one another, violating beds –the poor womem believing that they were receiving their husbands– and also treating their mothers and fathers as if they were enemies, and setting fire to houses. Thus they lost themselves in drunkenness. When the drinking was general and on the occasion of sacrifices everyone contributed towards it; when it was a private affair the host bore the expense with the help of his relatives. They make wine from honey, water and the root of a certain tree that they cultivated for this purpose. The drink thus produced was strong and smelled foul. When there were dances and festivities they would eat in twos or fours and after the meal the wine servers, who would not get drunk, brought great bowls to drink from until a general carouse ensued. The women took great care to get their drunken husbands home.

Often they spend on one banquet what they have earned in many days trading or scrounging. They have two ways of giving these feasts. The first, which is the manner of the chiefs and most important people, obliges each of the guests to give a similar banquet. Each of those invited must be given a roast bird, bread, and the cacao drink in plenty, and at the end of the feast, each is given a cloak to wear, a small stool and the most elegant drinking vessel the hosts can afford. If one of the guests dies, his household or his relatives have the obligation to provide the feast he owed. The other fashion is among relatives when they marry their children or commemorate the deeds if their ancestors. This does not require a feast in return, except that if an Indian has been invited to such a feast, so he invites all when he gives a banquet or marries his children. They think highly of friendship and conserve it, although they may be far apart, with these feasts. At these banquets, drink is served to them by beautiful women who, after passing the vessel, turn their back on the man who is drinking until it is empty.

The Indians have some most amusing entertainments, especially comic actors who perform with much grace. So good are they that the Spanish will hire some so that after observing the remarks of the Span-

Dances.

ish that pass by with their young ladies, of married couples or of themselves about good or bad service, they can later act this out with both
skill and accuracy.

They have small drums that they beat with the hand, and another
drum of hollow wood with a deep, mournful sound, that they strike
with a longish stick tripped with the gum of a certain tree. They have
long, slim trumpets of hollow wood with a long, twisted gourd at the
end, and they have another instrument that is a whole turtle with both
its shells; after taking out the flesh, they beat this with the palm of the
hand, and the sound of it is doleful and sad.

They have whistles of deer bone, and large conches, and reed flutes,
and with these instruments they play in honor of brave men.

They have two dances in particular that look very virile. The first
is a game with reeds, and so they call it *colomché*, which has this meaning. To perform it, the dancers form a large circle to the sound of the
music that accompanies them, and keeping time two of them leave the
circle. One holds a bundle of reeds and dances standing upright; the
other dances in a squatting position, both in time with the circle. The
one with the reeds throws them with all his might at the other, who
very skillfully snatches them from the air with a small rod. After this
they go back, keeping time, to the circle and others leave it to do the
same.

There is another dance in which 800 Indians, or more or fewer, take
part holding small flags, with the music and long steps of a war dance,
and not one is out of step. They dance slowly since they do not stop all
day, food and drink being taken to them. It was not the custom for
men to dance with women.

XXIII

Industry, trade and money.
Agriculture and seeds. Justice and hospitality.

The craftsmen among the Indians were potters and wood-carvers, who
earned much because they made idols of clay and wood, for which

they observed many fasts and rituals. There were also physicians, or rather sorcerers, who treated people using herbs and many superstitions, and also all the other occupations. The occupation they favored most was that of merchant, taking salt, clothing and slaves to the country of Ulúa and Tabasco, where they exchanged everything for cacao beans and stone beads that they used as money. With this currency they would buy slaves or finer and better beads that the chiefs wore as jewelry on festive occasions. For use as money or jewelry they also had others made from certain red seashells, which they carried in net pouches. In the markets they traded in all the many products of the country. They gave credit, lent and paid civilly and without interest.

The greatest in number were those who worked on the land and those who harvest maize and other seeds, which were stored in fine underground granaries or in cribs to sell in due time. Their mules and oxen are the people themselves. Customarily, for each married man and his wife, they would sow a plot 400 feet square that they call *hum uinic*, measured out with a twenty-foot rod, twenty feet wide and twenty feet long.

The Indians have the generous custom of helping one another in all their work. At the time of sowing, those who do not have any people of their own to carry out the task gather in groups of twenty, sometimes more or sometimes fewer, and all together complete the tilling, properly measured and calculated, of every one, and do not stop this work until all have been helped. Land, at the moment, is common, so the first to occupy it owns it. They sow crops in many places, so that if one fails, another will compensate. To prepare the land they simply cut down the brushwood and burn it, then sow. From the middle of January until April they tend the land, and sow when the rains begin. This they do carrying a small sack at their side, and using a pointed stick they make a hole in the earth, drop five or six grains into it which they cover using the same stick. It is amazing how they sprout up when it rains.

For hunting also they gather in groups of about fifty, and roast deer meat over sticks so that it will not spoil. On returning to the village, they make gifts of it to the chief and distribute what is left as friends; they to the same with the fishing catch.

The Indians, when they pay visits, always take with them a gift to present, according to their station; the person visited responds with another gift. Other persons present at these meetings speak and listen carefully, with respect to the person to whom they are speaking, though all address one another as "thou". In the course of the conversation, the person of lower rank will, out of respect, often repeat the position or title of the superior. They very often encourage those bringing messages with a breathing sound made in the throat that is as if to say "and then" or "and so". The women have little reasoning and do not usually speak for themselves, especially if they are poor, which is why the chiefs laughed at the friars, who listened to both rich and poor without distinction.

The wrongs they did to one another were redressed by the head of the offender's village; if not, it was the occasion and reason for more trouble. If they were from the same town they put the case before a judge, who was the person to decide. After examining the offense he would order satisfaction to be given; and if the offender lacked the means to do this, his friends and relatives would help. The usual causes for giving compensation were if they killed someone accidentally, or if a husband or wife commited suicide for some fault or for having given occasion for this, or when they were responsible for a fire that burned houses, land, beehives or grain cribs. Other injuries done out of wickedness were always settled with blood and fighting.

The Yucatecans are most generous and hospitable; no-one enters their houses but he is offered what food and drink they have: drink during the daytime and food at night. If they do not have anything they ask their neighbors. And on the road, if they are joined by others, they must share with all, even if they go short themselves as a result.

XXIV

How the Yucatecans count. Genealogies. Inheritances and guardianship of orphans. Succession of the chiefs.

They count by fives up to twenty, by twenties up to one hundred, by hundreds up to four hundred, and by four hundreds up to eight thousand. They used this method of counting much in buying and selling cacao. They have other very long counts that they extend ad infinitum, reckoning 8 thousand twenty times, making 160,000, then, using twenty again, multiply these 160,000 and continue multiplying in the same way until they come to an uncountable number. They make their calculations on the ground or on something flat.

They set much store on knowing the origin of their lineages, particularly if they belong to one of the houses of Mayapán. This they could learn from their priests, since it was one of their arts. They boast much about the distinguished men in their lineage. The father's name was passed on through their sons, but not daughters. Sons and daughters are always called by the name of both their father and mother, the father's as given name and the mother's as family name. Thus, the son of *Chel* and *Chan* was named *Nachanchel*, meaning the son of these people. This is why the Indians say that those with the same name are members of the family, and so treat them. Therefore, when they go to a place they do not know and find themselves in need, they will quickly make known their name, and if there is someone who bears the same, they are soon made welcome and treated generously. Therefore, no man or woman would marry someone with the same name, because for them it was very wicked. Now they call themselves both by their baptismal names and by the others.

The Indians did not allow daughters to inherit together with their brothers, save out of pity or goodwill, in which case they were given something and the rest the brothers divided equally among themselves, except that the one who had done most towards gaining property was given his reward. If all were daughters, the brothers or the next of kin inherited; and if they were not of an age for it to be wise to hand over the property, they gave it to a trustee, the nearest male relative, who gave the mother what was needed for his upbringing, as they were not accustomed to leave anything in the mother's control. Moreover, they would take the children away from their mothers, especially if the guardians were the brothers of the deceased. These guardians gave over everything they had received to the heirs, and not to do this was considered to be a great injustice and would be the reason for many disputes.

When they handed over the property it was in the presence of the chiefs and the most important men, when they took away what had been spent on their care and education. They did not give them any income from their lands except from bees and some cacao trees, saying that they had done enough in maintaining them.

If when the ruler died and his sons were not of an ag to govern but he had brothers, the eldest or the most capable ruled. They showed the heir their customs and ceremonies for when he came of age. These brothers, even when the heir was ready to rule controlled his life. If there were no brothers, the priests and the leading citizens elected a man suitable for the position.

XXV

Married couples. Divorce common among the Yucatecans. Marriage Customs.

Formerly, they used to marry when they were twenty years old, but now at the age of twelve or thirteen. Therefore they divorce more readily, because they marry withour love and ignorant of married life and of the duties of married men. If their parents could not persuade them to return to their wives, they would find them another and then another. Men with children left their wives just as easily, with no fear that another would take them as wives, or to return to them later. But nevertheless they are very jealous and will not tolerate their wives not being faithful; and now, because the Spanish kill their wives for this reason, they are beginning to mistreat and even kill them. If when they divorced their children were young, they left them with their mothers; if they were older, the boys went with their fathers and the girls with their mothers.

Although divorce was a common and familiar thing, the old people and those with better customs considered it bad, and there were many who had never had more than one wife. She was never from the father's family, because this was very bad in their eyes. If anyone married his sister-in-law, his brother's wife, this was also considered bad. They did not marry their step-mothers sisters-in-law (their wife's sisters) or aunts (their mother's sisters), and if a man did so, he was held to be

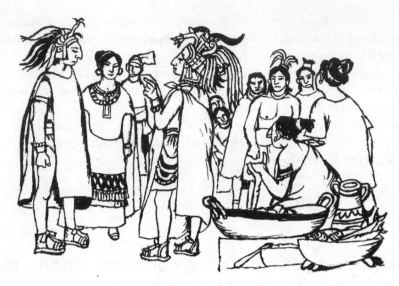

A wedding.

bad. They could marry all other female relatives on their mother's side, even a first cousin.

Fathers take great care to look for wives for their sons in good time, with status and position, if they could, in the same village. It was conisdered a disgrace to look for one's own wife, or for fathers to seek a match for their daughters. To arrange a marriage, they agreed on the marriage portion or settlement, which was very little, and the young man's father gave it to his son's future father-in-law. In addition to the dowry, the boy's mother made clothes for her daughter-in-law and son.

When the day of the marriage came, they gathered in the house of the girl's father, where a meal was prepared. Then came the guests and the priest, who brought the couple and their parents together and made sure they were in agreement and that the girl's parents had considered the boy carefully and were satisfied. Thus they gave the young man his wife for that night if all were agreed, then the feasting and celebration began. From that day on, the man lived in his father-in-law's house, working for him five or six years; if he did not work he was driven out of the house. The mothers made sure that the wife always gave her husband his food, as a sign of marriage.

Widows and widowers made their arrangements without celebrations or formalities; simply by going to a widow's house, being admitted and given a meal a man was considered married. The result was that they would leave each other as easily as they were united.

They Yucatecans never had more than a single wife, not as has been found in other regions where they have many at the same time. Sometimes parents arrange that their small children will be married when they are of age, and are treated as parents-in-law.

XXVI

Manner of baptizing in Yucatán. How it is celebrated.

There is no baptism in any part of the Indies except here in Yucatán, and it is even called by a word that means 'to be born anew or again,' which is the same as the Latin 'renascere'. For in the tongue of Yucatán, *zihil* means 'to be born anew or again,' but is used only in composite forms, thus *caputzihil* means 'to be reborn.'

We have not been able to learn the origin of baptism, only that it is a custom they have always had and for which they held such devotion that there is no-one who does not undergo it. They had such reverence for it that those who had sinned, or who knew they were about to do so, had to make these sins known, especially to the priests. They had such faith in this ceremony that they would never repeat the sin. What they believed they received through baptism was an inherent disposition to be good in their ways and protection against demons in earthly matters, and that through it and their good life, they would enter the paradise they hoped for where, like in the one of Mahomet, they would have food and drink in plenty.

This was their custom for preparing for baptism: the Indian women brought up the children until the age of three. They always put a large white bead on the heads of the boys, fastened to the hair on the crown. The girls were encircled about their hips by a thin cord with a small shell attached to it that covered their private parts. It was considered a

Maya baptism.

sin and wicked thing to remove the token of the girls before baptism, which they always performed on them between the ages of three and twelve; they never married before baptism.

When someone wished to have his child baptized, he went to see the priest and told him of his intention. The priest announced the baptism to the town, and they always made sure that the day chosen for it was not ill-omened. When this was done, the man who was giving the feast, who was the one to head all discussions, selected the leading man of the town he wanted to help him in the matter and the things he had to do. It was their custom then to choose four more old and respected men to assist the priest at the ceremony on the day of the feast; these were chosen together with the priest. The fathers of all the children who were going to be baptized took part in making the selections, since the celebration was for all. The men they chose were called *chacs*. For three days before the ceremony, the children's fathers and those officiating fasted and abstained from women.

On the day they all assembled in the house of the one who was giving the feast, and took all the children who were to be baptized. These were all placed in order in the court or courtyard of the house, which was ready cleaned and scattered with fresh leaves, the boys on one side and the girls on the other. An old woman was made protectoress of the girls and a man put in charge of the boys.

This done, the priest proceeded with the purification of the house, casting the evil spirit from it. To expel it, four small benches were placed in the corners of the courtyard on which sat the four *chacs*, with a cord tied from one to the other so that the children were confined inside it. Then, all the children's fathers, who had fasted, had to enter the enclosure by stepping over the cord. After or before this, they placed another bench in the center where the priest sat, with a brazier, a little ground maize, and a little incense. Then the boys and girls went up to him in line, and the priest put a small quantity of maize and incense into their hands, which all of them threw onto the brazier. This purification of the air done, they took away the brazier on which it had been perfomed and the cord with which the *chacs* held the children surrounded. They poured a little wine into a drinking cup and gave everything to an Indian for him to carry out of the village, warning him not to drink or to look behind him as he returned. They said that with this the demon was expelled.

When the Indian had left they cleared the courtyard of leaves, which were of a tree they had called *cihom*, and threw down others from another tree that they called *copó*, and spread some mats while the priest was putting on his ceremonial attire. When clothed, he came out wearing a tunic of red feathers embroidered with different colored feathers and long plumes hanging from the edges. On his head he wore a sort of cone of the same feathers, and below the tunic many cotton ribbons that hung down to the ground like tails. He held a water sprinkler made of a short, richly carved rod which had as fringes or tassels the tails of a certain sepent that are like rattles. He bore himself with the dignity of a pope about to crown an emperor, and the awe that this apparel caused among those present was amazing. Then, the *chacs* approached the children and placed on the head of each one a white cloth that their mothers brought for this purpose. They asked the older children if they had committed any sin or given any lewd caresses, and if they had they confessed and were separated from the others.

This done, the priest ordered all to be silent and to be seated, and then with great solemnity began to bless the children using many incantations, and to bless them with his sprinkler. When he had blessed them he sat dowm and the man chosen by all the children's fathers to lead the celebration would rise and, with a bone given to him by the priest, strike each one nine times on the forehead. Then he dipped the bone into a vessel of liquid he carried and anointed them on the fore-head, the face, between their toes and fingers without a word. This water was made of certain flowers and of cacao steeped and mixed in 'virgin water' as they called it, collected from hollows in the trees or rocks of the forests.

After this anointment, the priest stood and removed the white cloths from their heads and others they had on their backs in which each one carried a few feathers of very beautiful birds and some cacao beans, all of which one of the *chacs* collected. Then using a stone knife, the priest cut off the bead that the boys had worn on their heads. After this, the priest's assistants came up with a posy of flowers and a pipe such as the Indians smoke and with each of these threatened the children nine times. Then they gave them the flowers to smell and the pipe to smoke. Then they collected the gifts that the mothers had provided and from them gave each child something to eat, for the offerings were of food. They took a good cup of wine and offered the rest of the gifts to the gods entreating them devoutly to accept this small offering from the children. And calling on another official who was assisting, called *cayom*; they gave him wine to drink, which he did tirelessly, which may be called a sin.

When this was done, the girls were the first to leave, whose moth-ers removed the cord they had worn over their hips until then and the shell over their viginity. This was as sign that they could be married whenever their parents wished. After, the children were sent away and their fathers went to the pile of cloaks they had brought and each with his own hand distributed them to the assistants and officials. The cel-ebration ended with plentiful eating and drinking. They called this feast *emku*, which means 'the descent of the god'. The man who had been mainly responsible for it, arranging everything and bearing the cost, in addition to the three days of continence he had observed as part of his fast had to contain himself for nine days more, which was observed invariably.

XXVII

A sort of confession among the Yucatecans. Abstinence and superstitions. The variety and great number of idols. Duties of the priests.

The Yucatecans knew instinctively when they were doing wrong and, because they believed that death, disease and sufferings came to them as a result of wrongdoing and sin, they used to confess when these were upon them. Therefore, when they were in danger of death through disease or another thing, they would confess their sins, and if they neglected to do this their nearest relatives or friends would remind them; and then they recounted them, to the priest if he was there, and if not, to their mothers and fathers, women to their husbands and men to their wives.

The sins of which they generally accused themselves were theft, homicide, those of the flesh, and false witness, and with this they believed themselves saved. Many times, if they escaped death, there were quarrels between husbands and wives because of any dishonour that had been brought on them, and with the men or women who had caused it.

Men confessed their transgressions, except with their female slaves, those who had any, because they said that they had the right to make use of their possessions as they wished. They did not confess sins of intention, although they considered them to be bad and in their counsellings and preachings advised avoiding them,

The abstinences they commonly observed were from salt and chili pepper in their food, which was arduous for them. They abstained from their wives before celebrating all their feasts.

They did not marry until a year after being widowed, having no relations with a man or a woman during this time. They considered those who did not observe this custom to be intemperate, and believed that some ill would befall them as a result.

During some fasts for their celebrations, they neither ate meat nor had relations with their wives. They always undertook their duties at festivities after fasting, and similarly when they were given State duties. Some fasts were so long that they lasted three years, and it was a great sin to break them.

They were so given to their idolatrous prayers that in times of need even women, boys and girls took part in burning incense, praying their god to deliver them from the evil and defeat the demon that was causing it.

Even travelers took incense with them on their journeys and a small plate on which to burn it. Thus, at night, wherever they reached, they set down three small stones, putting a little incense on each, and in front of them three flat stones on which they burned the incense, praying to the god they call *Ek-chuah* that he bring them safely back to their homes. This they did every night until they were in their homes once more, where someone had always done the same for them, or more.

They had a great host of idols and of temples that were sumptuous in their own way. And apart from these communal temples, the lord priests and the most important people had shrines and idols in their houses for their private prayers and offerings. They held *Cuzmil* and the well at *Chicheniztá* in such great veneration as we do pilgrimages to Jeruralem and Rome. Therefore they used to go and visit them to make offerings, especially to *Cuzmil*, as we go to holy places. And when they did not go, they always sent their offerings. Those who went also used to enter the derelict temples as they passed by them to pray and burn *copal* incense.

The idols of their gods were not enough for them, so many did they have; there were no animals or insects of which they did not make statues, and they made all of them into gods and goddesses. They had a few stone idols, and small sized ones of wood, but not so many as clay ones. The wood idols were so highly prized that they were passed down as the most valuable part of an inheritance. They had no metal idols because there is no metal in the region. They knew very well that the idols were their own works and so lifeless and without the divine breath, but they were revered for what they represented and because their making involved many ceremonies, especially the wooden ones.

The most idolatrous were the priests, *chilanes*, sorcerers and physicians, *chaces* and *nacones*. They duty of the priests was to deal in and teach their lore; to indicate their needs and their solutions; to forecast and date celebrations; make sacrifices and administer their sacraments. The work of the *chilanes* was to announce to the town the pronouncements of their demon gods, and they were held in such high esteem that they were sometimes carried on shoulders. The sorcerers and physicians healed by bleeding from where the patient had pain, and would cast omens in this and in other things. The *chaces* were four old men always chosen on each occasion to help the priest to perform the ceremonies correctly and fully. The *Nacones* were two officials: one was permanent and had little prestige, since it was he who cut open the chests of the people who were sacrificed: the other was a leader chosen for war and for festivals. This office lasted for three years and was a great honor.

XXVIII

Sacrifices and the cruel and obscene self-mortifications of the Yucatecans. Human victims put to death with arrows.

The men made sacrifices of their own blood, sometimes cutting into the edges of their ears at intervals all around, and they left them like this as a sign. Sometimes they pierced their cheeks or lower lip, made incisions in other parts of the body, or would pierce their tongues from side to side and run straws through the hole, which was extremely painful. A times they tore the skin at the end of their member into shreds, leaving it in the same state as their ears, which led the official historian of the Indies to say wrongly that they practiced circumcision.

Sometimes they carried out a foul and laborious sacrifice. Those who were performing it assembled in the temple and, standing in a row, each made a hole through his member from side to side; then they passed throgh the greatest quantity of cord they could, and so all were threaded through. The also used the blood of all to anoint those same parts of the demon, and the more a man did this, the more valiant he was considered. Their sons began to do this from an early age, and it is dreadful to see how zealous they are.

It was not the custom of the women to shed their blood, although they worhiped the images with fervor, but they would instead anoint

Scarification

the face of the demon with the blood of the birds of the air, the animals of the earth and the fish of the waters and any other thing they could obtain. Other things they offered. They took the hearts of some animals and offered that, some they offered whole; some alive, some dead; some raw, some cooked. They also made great offerings of bread and wine and all the kinds of food and drink that they had.

For marking these sacrifices, there were tall, carved wooden posts standing in the temple courts; near the temple steps was a broad, round pedestal with a rather thin stone four or five palms high standing at the center. At the top of the steps was another such pedestal.

Apart from at festivals, which they solemnized by sacrificing animals, the priest or the *chilanes* would demand human sacrifice in the case of some great tribulation or need, to which all contributed. Some gave the means for buying slaves and others, out of devotion, handed over their young children. These were indulged until their day and feast came, but closely guarded so that they could not escape or else defile themselves with some sin of the flesh. And while they were being taken from town to town with dances, the priests fasted, together with the *chilanes* and the officials.

When the day for the ceremony came, they gathered in the temple court, and if the victim was to be sacrificed with arrows they stripped him completely, painted his body blue and placed a cone-shaped cap on his head. After the ceremony of casting out the evil spirit, all the people performed a solemn dance with him around the pole, all holding bows and arrows. Still dancing, they took hold of him and bound him, as they all danced and watched him. Then the unholy priest came up in his robes and with an arrow wounded the victim, whether man or woman, in the private parts. He drew blood, then came down and with it smeared the face of the demon. At a certain sign from him the dancers, as if dancing, passed by him quickly and in an orderly fashion and began to loose arrows at his heart, which was shown by a white mark. In this way, the point on his chest soon bristled with arrows.

If his heart was to be taken out they brought him to the court with great show and a large company of people. When he had been painted blue and the cap placed on his head he was taken to the round stone that was the sacrificial altar. After the priest and his assistants had anointed the stone with the blue coloring and cast out the evil spirit, purifying the temple, the *chaces* seized the poor creature they were sacrificing, very swiftly laid him on his back on the stone and took hold of his arms and legs, which they spread. At this, the *nacón* executioner approached with a stone knife and very skillfully made a cruel incision between the ribs on the left side, just below the nipple. Then he reached in and, seizing the heart like a ravening tiger, tore out the living heart. This he gave to the priest on a plate who hurried to anoint the faces of the idols with the fresh blood.

Sometimes they performed this sacrifice on the stone on the top step of the temple and then would set the body to roll down the staircase. At the bottom, the officials took the body and flayed it completely except the hands and feet, then the naked priest wrapped himself in this skin and all the others danced with him. This was an occasion of great solemnity for them. These victims were commonly buried in the courtyard of the temple or, if not, were eaten, being distributed among the chiefs and those they were sufficient for. The hands, feet and heads were for the priests and the officials. The victims thus sacrificed were regarded as sanctified. If they were slaves taken prisoner in war their masters would take their bones to use them as insignia during their dances, as a sign of victory. Sometimes, they threw living persons into the well at *Chichenizá*, believing that they came out on the third day, even though they never appeared again.

XXIX

Weapons of the Yucatecans. Military leaders. Drafted troops and regular soldiers; the customs of war.

They have weapons for offense and defense. The offensive ones were bows, and arrows carried in quivers with heads of flint, and very sharp fish teeth, which they shoot very skillfully and strongly. The bows are made of a beautiful tawny wood, marvellously strong, and more straight than curved; the strings are made of native hemp. The length of the bow is always a little less than the height of the one who carries it. The arrows are made with some very slender canes that grow in the lagoons and more than five palms in length; they tie to the cane a thin piece of very strong wood into which the flint is inserted. It was not their custom to tip their arrows with poison, nor do they know about this, although they had them in abundance. They had ax-heads of a certain metal in this shape [see illustration], which they fitted into a wooden shaft, and these served them as both weapons and tools for carving wood. They sharpened them by beating them with a stone, since the metal is soft. They had short spears as high as a man with heads of very hard flint. They had no other weapons for attack but these.

To defend themselves they had round shields made of tightly woven split canes covered with deerskin. They made quilted tunics with two layers of brine-soaked cotton padding, and these were very resistant. Some leaders and captains, but not many, wore a sort of helmet made of wood; and with these arms, wearings plumes and tiger and lion skins those who had them, they went to war.

Maya warriors,

They always had two captains, one permanent, whose post was hereditary, and another who was elected for three years with many ceremonies either to arrange the feast they celebrated in their month of *Pax*, on May 12, or as commander of the men recruited for war.

This commander was called *Nacón*, and during these three years he could not have relations with any woman, not even his own wife, or eat meat. They respected him greatly and supplied him with fish and iguanas, which are like lizards, to eat. He did not get drunk during this time and in his house the vessels and things he used were kept separate. No woman was in his service, and he had little contact with the town. After the three years he lived as before.

These two captains dealt with matters of war and organized everything. For this, there were men chosen as soldiers who, when it was necessary, presented themselves with their arms. These were called *holcanes*, and if they were not enough, others were assembled whom the captains agreed to divide between themselves. Led by a tall banner, they would leave the town very quietly and thus go to attack their enemies marcilessly, uttering loud war-cries, wherever they came upon them unawares.

On the roads and in passes, the enemy erected defensive positions for archers of stakes and wood or often of stone. After a victory they severed the jawbones from the dead and, having cleaned them of flesh, hung them on their arms. They made great offerings of the spoils for their war, and if they took an important man prisoner they sacrificed him at once because they did not wish to leave anyone alive who could later harm them. The rest of those taken prisoner belonged to whoever captured them.

These *holcanes* were given no payment except in times of war, and when there was war the captains gave them a certain amount of money, but little because it came out of their own; if they did not have enough, the town contributed towards it. The town also supplied them with food, which the women prepared for them. They carried it on their own backs, having no pack animals, and for this reason wars lasted a very short time. When the war was over the soldiers, while the battle spirit still reigned and with this as a pretext, made great impositions on their towns, demanding to be served and regaled. If one of them had killed a captain or chief he was greatly honored and feted.

XXX

The penalties and punishments for adulterers, murderers and thieves. The education of young men. The custom of flattening children's heads.

These people had the custom, inherited from Mayapán, of punishing adulterers in the following manner: when an investigation had been made and a man convicted of adultery, the leading men gathered in the chief's house. The adulterer was brought to them and they tied him to a stake and handed him to the husband of the offending woman. If he pardoned him, he was free; if not he killed him by dropping a large stone on his head from a high place. For the woman, the great infamy was punishment enough, and usually they were abandoned because of this.

The penalty for killing a person, even by accident, was to be taken by his relatives or, if not, to pay blood money. Theft, even a small one, was paid for and punished by enslavement, and this is why there were so many slaves, especially in times of hunger. For this reason, we friars worked so much on baptism, so that they would be given their freedom. If the thief was a chief or leader, the town assembled and the culprit was scarified on both sides of the face from chin to forehead as punishment, which they considered a great dishonor.

Young men had great respect for the elders and took their advice, so men boasted of being old and told the young men about what they had experienced, which they had to believe. If the young men followed their advice, the old men were respected more highly. The old men were held in so much awe that the young approached them only on matters of the utmost importance, for example if they were about to marry. They had very little to do with married men. Because of this, it was the custom to have in each town a large, lime-washed house open on all sides where the young men would gather for their passtimes. They played ball, and a game like dice using knucklebones, and many others. They generally slept here all together until they married.

And though I have heard that in other parts of the Indies they indulged in unnatural practices in these houses, I have not heard that they do so in this country. And I do not think they did, because those who practice this foul vice are said to have no taste for women as these had. For they used to take whores to these places and there use them, and the miserable women among this people who led this life, though receiving payment from the youths, were used by so many that they were harassed and even died.

They daubed themselves with black coloring and did not use to be tattooed, except lightly, until they were married. In all other things they accompanied their fathers and so became great idol-worshipers just like them and helped them in their works.

The Indian women raised their children very harshly and kept them completely naked. Four or five days after the child was born, they laid it face down on a small bed made of rods and put its head between two boards; one over the back and one over the forehead. They bound these and left the child there suffering until after a few days the head was flattened and shaped in the way they all had them. The pain and the danger was so great for the children that some almost died, and the present writer saw the head of one burst open behind the ears; the boards must do this to many.

They were raised completely naked, except that at the age of four or five they were given a sleeping wrap and the boys some strips of cloth to cover themselves like their fathers, and they began to cover the girls from the waist down. They were nursed for a long time, for the mothers gave them milk for as long as they could, even if they were four or five years old; as a result there are so many strong, healthy people among them.

For the first two years they grew wonderfully pretty and plump. Afterward, with their mother's continual bathing and the sun they darkened, but throughout their childhood they were attractive and lively, always carrying bow and arrows and playing with one another. Thus they grew until they began to behave as adolescents, taking themselves more seriously and abandoning their childhood ways.

XXXI

Clothing and ornaments of the Indian women of Yucatán

In general, the women of Yucatán are of better build than Spanish women, larger and better formed, but they do not have such wide hips as negresses. Those who are beautiful are proud of it, and indeed they are not unhansome; they are not fair-skinned, but brown, which is caused by the sun and constant bathing rather than being natural. They do not paint their faces as the women of our country do, for they consider this immoral. They used to file their teeth, leaving them like the teeth of a saw, and this they consider elegant. Some old women perform this duty, filing with certain stones and water.

They pierced the their noses through the cartilage dividing the nostrils to put a piece of amber in the hole as an ornament. They pierced their ears so as to wear ornaments just as their husbands did; they tattooed their bodies from the waist up –except the breasts, because of nursing– with designs that were more delicate and beautiful than those of the men. They bathed very frequently with cold water, like the men do, and not with over much modesty, because they would strip naked at the well where they went to take water for bathing. They also used to bathe with water heated over a small fire, but more for health reasons than for cleanliness.

Like their husbands, they used to rub themselves with a red ointment, and those who could afford it used a certain preparation of a very sticky aromatic gum that I think is liquidamber and which they call *iztah-te* in their language.They spread this on a special stone shaped like a cake of soap that was carved with elegant designs, and with this applied the gum to their breasts, arms and backs, which leaves them elegant and sweet-smelling, or so they believe. If the ointment was good, it lasted a long time without wearing off.

They wore their hair very long and used to, and still do, arrange it in a very becoming fahion, parted down the center, or they braided it for another style. When girls are about to be married, methodical mothers dress their hair with such skill that I have seen many Indian girls with hairstyles as elaborate as those of fashionable Spanish women. Until the girls are more grown up their hair is braided into two or four plaits, which look very well on them.

The Indian women of Bacalar and Campeche are very modest in their dress, for in addition to the covering they wore from the waist down they covered their breasts, drawing them to the side under a folded cloth. All the others wore only a garment like a long, wide sack, open at the sides and reaching to the hips, where they tied the bottom ends together. They had no other article of clothing except the cloak in which they always sleep. When they were traveling, they used to carry this folded or rolled up and covered.

XXXII

The chastity and behavior of the Indian women of Yucatán. Their chief qualites and their household economy. Their devoutness and the special customs at childbirth.

The women prided themselves on being chaste, and they had good reason for this because, as the old now lament, before they knew us Spaniards they were extremely virtuous, and I shall give two instances of this. Captain Alonso López de Avila, brother-in-law of governor Montejo captured an Indian girl, a handsome, gentle woman, in the war at Bacalar. She, in fear that she would not be killed in the war, had promised her husband that she would know no other man but him. And for this reason she could not be persuaded not to take her own life for fear of being defiled by another man. Because of this, she was thrown to the dogs.

An Indian woman who was about to be baptized came to me to complain about a baptized man who was in love with her for her beauty. He waited until her husband was away, then went to her house one night, and after making his intentions clear by his wooing, to no avail, he tried to offer her gifts he had brought for the purpose. When this also failed, he tried to force her, and as he was a big, strong man he tried all night, but all he won from her was such great anger that she came to me to complain about the Indian's wickedness; this is what she reported.

The women would turn their backs to the men when they met them anywhere, and made way for them to pass; the same when they gave them to drink, they would turn away until they had finished. They teach their daughters what they know, and bring them up well in their own ways, scolding them, instructing them and making them work; if they erred they punished them by pinching their ears or arms. If mothers see their daughters raise their eyes they reprove them severely and put native pepper on them which is extremely painful. If they behave immodestly they whip them and apply pepper to another part of their bodies as punishment and humiliation. As an insult and serious repri-

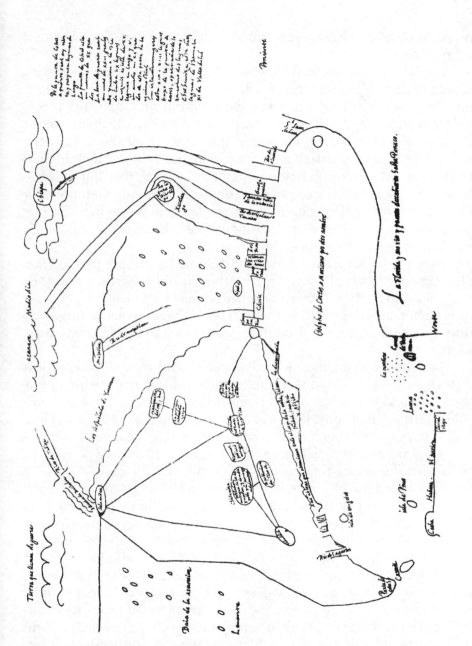

The peninsula. Another map of Yucatán that also appears in the Account.

mand to unruly girls they say that they appear to have been brought up motherless.

Women are jealous, and some of them to such a degree that they would lay hands on the person who was the cause of their jealousy; also, they were so quick-tempered and resentful, although very meek, that they would twist their husband's hair if they made them jealous occasionally. They are hard workers and very capable housekeepers, for on them rest the greatest and most tasks in maintaining their homes, raising their children and paying taxes. And with all this, if it is necessary they assume even more work, plowing and sowing their plots for food. They are excellent earners, working late into the night in the few moments they have left after their household duties and going to the markets to buy and sell their things.

They raise both native and Spanish birds to sell and to eat. They also raise birds for pleasure and for their feathers, with which they make elegant clothes. They raise other domestic animals, and of these they suckle the deer, making them so tame that they never run away into the woodlands even though they are taken to and fro and raised there.

They help one another in weaving cloth and repay this work just as their husbands repay that of their lands. And as they are doing this they joke and tell stories about their husbands, and sometimes complain a little. They consider it very unseemly to look at the men and laugh at them, and therefore this alone was enough to give insult, and bring the women into disgrace without further ado. They performed their own dances by themselve. and some with the men, especially one they called *Naual*, which is rather immodest. They are very fertile, bear children very early and are excellent nurses, for two reasons: first, their morning drink, which they take hot, produces a great quantity of milk,and second, the constant grinding of maize, with their breasts loose makes them grow very large and so hold a lot of milk.

They too used to get drunk at feasts, although since they ate apart, not so much as the men. They desire to have many children, and the woman who did not have any used to implore the idols for them, offering gifts and prayers; now they beg them of God.They are prudent and courteous, sociable with the people who can understand them, and wonderfully generous. They have few secrets and are very clean in their persons and in their habits since they wash like ermines do.

They were very devout and pious, and so paid much attention to their idols, burning incense and offering gifts of cotton clothing, food and drink. It was also their duty to prepare the offerings of food and drink that were made at the Indians' feasts. But despite all this, they did not follow the custom of shedding their blood in honor of the idols, and never did this. Nor were they allowed into the temples when sacrifices were being made, except at certain festivals some old women were admitted to the act. For childbirth they were helped by the sorceresses, who made them believe their lies and put the image of a demon called *Ixchel* under the bed, for they said that she was the goddess who created children.

When children were born they were bathed immediately, and when they were released from the torture of having their heads and foreheads flattened, they were taken before the priest for him to cast their fate, say what occupation the child should have, and give him the name he would bear during his childhood. This was because they used to give children different names until they were baptized or were more grown up; afterwards, these were abandoned and they began to be called by their fathers' name until they were married, when they took the names of both father and mother.

XXXIII

Mourning. Burials of the priests. Statues for holding the ashes of chiefs. The reverence paid to these. Beliefs about the afterlife.

These people had a great, excessive fear of death and demonstrated this in all the things they did for their gods, which were for nothing else but to be rewarded with health, life and food. But when they came to die, the lamentations and weeping for their dead and the grief they caused them were something to see. They mourned them silently by day, but at night with loud and most piteous cries that were painful to hear. They went about in extreme sadness for many days. They observed abstinences and fasts for the deceased person, especially for a

Funerary urn.

husband or wife, and said that the devil had carried him off, since they believed that all evils, particularly death, came upon them from him.

They wrapped the dead in a shroud, filling their mouths with ground maize, their food, and a drink that they call *koyem*, together with some of those stones that they use as money, so that they would not lack food in the afterlife. They were buried either inside their house or behind them, and some of their idols were throw into the grave; if he was a priest, some of his books, if a sorcerer, his divining stones and other belongings. They would usually abandon the house and leave it empty after a burial except when there were a lot of people living in it, in whose company they would lose some of the fear the death left them with.

They cremated the bodies of chiefs and high-ranking people and placed their ashes in urns, and built temples over them, as those found at *Izamal* show was done in former times. Nowadays, they have been found to put the ashes in hollow clay statues when the dead were great chiefs.

Other high-ranking people made wooden statues for their fathers in which they left a hollow in the back of the head; some part of the body was cremated and the ashes placed there and sealed in. Then they took the skin off the back of the skull and fastened it there, burying the rest of the corpse in the usual way; they kept these statues very reverently among their idols. When *Cocom* chiefs died in ancient times they cut off their heads, which were boiled and cleaned of flesh, then the back half of the skull was sawn off, leaving the front with the jaws and teeth. The flesh missing from these half skulls was replaced with a special paste, with which they reproduced perfectly the features of the person whose skull it was. These were kept with the statues containing ashes, all in the shrines of their houses with their idols, and held in great reverence and respect. On all their feast days and celebrations they made offerings to them of food so that they would not be without in the afterlife where they believed their souls came to rest and their gifts were appreciated.

These people have always believed in the immortality of the soul, more than many other nations, although they have not been so civilized. They believed that after death there was another, better life that the soul enjoyed after it left the body. They said that this future life was divided into good and bad, into suffering and peace. The evil life full of suffering, they said, was for the wicked; the good and pleasurable one for those who had led virtuous lives. The reward they said they would receive if they were good was to go to a most delightful place where nothing would cause them sorrow and where there would be rich food and drink in abundance, and a cool, shady tree that they call *yaxché* (the silk-cotton tree), in the shade of whose branches they would all rest and be in peace forever.

The torments of the evil life that they said awaited the wicked were to go to a place that was lower than the other, called *mitnal*, which means hell, and to be tortured by demons, by great hunger, cold, exhaustion and sadness. In this place there was also a demon, the prince of all the demons whom they all obeyed; he was called *Hunhau* in their tongue. They said that these good and bad lives had no end, since the soul had no end. They also said, and were completely sure of it, that those who hanged themselves went to this paradise; therefore, there were many who in times of unimportant troubles of sadness, hardship or sickness hanged themselves in order to escape from them and go to rest in paradise where, they said, *Ixtab*, the goddess of the noose would come to take them. They had no notion of the resurrection of the body, and could not explain who had told them of this paradise and hell of theirs.

XXXIV

The reckoning of the Yucatecan year. The symbols of the days. The four Bacabs and Their names. The days of ill omen.

The sun in this land of Yucatàn never hides nor goes so far away for the nights to be longer than the days; when they are at their longest, from St. Andrew's day to St. Lucia's day [Nov. 20-Dec. 13] they are equal, then the days begin to lengthen. To tell the time at night the Indians guided themselves by the evening star [Venus], the Pleiades, and Castor and Pollux. During the daytime their point of reference was noon, and with that they had given names to periods of time from sunrise and until sunset according to which they organized themselves and arranged their work.

They had their perfect year like ours of 365 days and 6 hours, and they divide it into two kinds of months. Some have 30 days, which they call *U*, meaning moon and they counted them from when the moon first rose until it disappeared. They had the other type of month with 20 days, which they call *Uinal Hunekeh*, and the complete year had 18 of these, plus five days and six hours. With these six hours they made an extra day every four years, and so from the four parts had a year of 366 days every fouth year. For these 360 days they have 20 letters or symbols to name them, leaving the other five without names because they were considered ill-omened and evil. The symbols are those that follow, and each one has its name below written as in our own language so that it may be understood.

I have already told that the Indians' way of counting is in fives, and that with four fives they make twenty. So, from these symbols of theirs, which represent 20, they take the first one from each of the four

Kan   Chicchan   Cimi   Manik   Lamat

Muluc   Oc   Chuen   Eb   Ben

Ix   Men   Cib   Caban   Ezanab

Cauac   Ahau   Imix   Ik   Akbal

sets of five in the 20, and each one of these serves as do our Dominical letters to designate the first day of each twenty-day month.

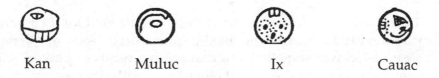

Kan   Muluc   Ix   Cauac

Among the multitude of gods that these people worshiped there were four that were each called B*acab*. These, they said, were four brothers that God placed at the four corners of the world when he created it to hold up the sky so that it would not fall. They also relate about these *bacabs* that they escaped when the world was destroyed by the deluge. They give each of these a separate name, and use these to name the part of the world where god placed him to support the sky, also taking one of the four Dominical letters for him and for the part where he stands. They also know what good or evil to expect from every year corresponding to these figures and their accompanying letters.

And the evil one, who has deceived them in this as in all the rest, told them what services and offerings they had to give to protect themselves from hard times. So, if these did not befall them they said that it was because of the ceremonies that had benn performed; but if they did come, the priests told and convinced the people that it was because of some error or defect in the ceremonies or of those who performed them,

So then, the first of these Dominical letters is *Kan*. The year indicated by this symbol was under the sign of the *Bacab* they called by several names: *Hobnil, Kanalbacab, Kanpauahtun* or *Kanxibchac*. To him was assigned the South. The second symbol is Muluc, assigned to the East, and the year was governed by the *Bacab* called *Canzienal, Chacalbacab, Chacpauahtun* or *Chacxibchac*. The third symbol is *Ix*, and this year corresponded to the *Bacab* called *Zaczini, Zacalbacab, Zacpauahtun* or *Zacxibchac*, and was North. The fourth symbol is *Cauac*: this year was under the *Bacab* called *Hozanek, Ekelbacab, Ekpauahtun* and *Ekxibchac*; this was West.

Kan   Muluc   Ix   Cauac

In any feast or solemn ceremony these people held for their gods they always began by expelling the evil spirit so as to perform it better. This expulsion was sometimes carried out by means of prayers and blessing especially for this and at other times with ceremonies, offerings and sacrifices for the purpose. To honor the solemn celebration of the New Year more joyfully and worthily, according to these deluded people, they did not work during the five days they considered unlucky before the first day of their New Year and in this time held great ceremonies for the *bacabs* mentioned above and for the devil, to whom they gave four different names: *Kanuuayayab, Chacuuayayab, Zacuuayayab* and *Ekuuayayab*. With these ceremonies and feasts over, and the evil spirit driven out, they began their new year as we shall now see.

XXXV

Festivals during the ill-omened days. Sacrifices for the new year of the symbol *Kan.*

In all the towns of Yucatán it was customary to have two piles of stones, one opposite the other at the gateway to the town and also in the four quarters of it, namely east, west, north and south for celebrating the two feasts in the unlucky days that were celebrated each year in the same manner.

The year whose Dominical letter was *Kan* was governed by *Hobnil*, and, according to what they say, both of these ruled the South. This year, then, they made a hollow clay image or figure of the evil god they called *Kanuuayayab* and carried it to the pile of dry stones they had in the southern quarter. They would choose a leader of the town in whose house the feast days would be celebrated, and to do this they used to make a statue of the evil spirit they called *Bolonzacab*, which they placed in the house of the master of ceremonies in a place that was open to all.

This done, the chiefs and the priest, together with the men of the town assembled and, with the path to the pile of stones where the statue stood cleaned and decorated with arches and foliage, they walked along it all together very devoutly. When they reached the statue the priest censed it with forty-nine grains of maize ground up with incense, and the others threw this into the brazier of the demon idol and perfumed it. The ground maize alone they called *zacah*, and that of the chiefs *chahalté*. They perfumed the image, then cut the head off a fowl and offered it up to the statue.

This done they put the image on a pole called *kanté*, putting an angel on its back as a sign of water, meaning that this year would be a good one; and they painted these angels to look frightening. Thus they bore it with great rejoicing and dancing to the house of the chief where the other statue of *Bolonzacab* stood. From the house of the master of the ceremony they brought to the road a drink made of 415 grains of roasted maize that they call *piculakakla* for the chiefs and priests, of which they all drank. On arriving at the house of the head of festivities they placed the image opposite the statue of the demon that was there and then made many offerings of food and drink, of meat and fish. These offerings were divided among any strangers who were present, and to the priest they gave a leg of venison.

Others shed blood by cutting their ears and with it anointed a stone image they had there of the demon *Kanalacantun*. They would fashion a heart out of bread and another of pumpkin seeds and offer them to the image of the demon *Kanuuayayab*. Thus they kept the statue and image during the fateful days and perfumed them with their incense mixed with ground maize. They believed that if they did not perform these rites they were sure to suffer from certain of their sicknesses in that year. When the ill-omened days were past they took the statue of the demon *Bolonzacab* to the temple and the image to the eastern quarter, where they would go for it the following year. They left it there and went to their homes, each to occupy himself with what remained to him to do in the celebrations for the new year.

The ceremonies over and the evil spirit exorcised according to their false beliefs, they regarded this year as good, since the *bacab Hobnil* governed it under the letter *Kan*. Of him they said that he had not sinned like his brothers, and so under him no evil would befall them. But, because misfortune often came, this evil god also established that they should perform rites in his honor so that when they were afflicted they could lay the blame on the celebrations or celebrants, and thus remain forever deluded and blinded.

Therefore, he ordered them to make an idol that they called *Yzamnakauil* and to place it in their temple and in the court of the temple to burn three balls of a milk or resin called *kik* [latex]. They should also sacrifice a dog or a man to him, which they did in the manner they have already been described as using for whatever they sacrificed, except that the fashion of execution was different for this festival. In the courtyard of the temple they built a great pile of stones and placed the man or dog they were going to sacrifice on something higher. After throwing the bound victim from on high on to the stones, the attendants seized him and swiftly tore out his heart, which they then took and offered to the new idol between two plates. They offered other gifts of food, and in this festival old women of the town who were specially chosen danced wearing certain clothes. They said that an angel descended and received this sacrifice.

XXXVI

Sacrifices for the new year *Muluc*. Dances on stilts. Dance of the old women carrying clay dogs.

The year in which the Dominical letter was *Muluc* was governed by *Canzienal*, and at this time the chiefs and the priest elected a master of ceremonies. After this, they made the image of the evil god as they had done the previous year, which they named *Chacuuayayab*, and this they carried to the pile of stones in the East where they had left the idol of the year before. They made a statue of the demon called *Kinchahau* and set it in the house of the headman in a suitable place, and from there they walked along a well-cleaned and decorated road all together with their accustomed devotion to fetch the image of the demon *Chacuuayayab*.

When they reached it the priest perfumed the image with fifty grains of maize ground with that incense of theirs, which they call *zacah*. The priest gave to the lords another incense that we call *chahalté* to throw on to the brazier. Then they cut the head off a fowl, just as they did for the other image and, taking the idol on a pole called *chasté*, they carried it, all showing great reverence and performing certain wardances that they call *holcanokot batelokot*. For the lords and leaders, their drink made of 380 grains of toasted maize was brought out to their progress as on the previous occasion.

When they reached the house of the president of ceremonies they placed this image opposite the statue of *Kinchahau* and made all their offerings, which they distributed as before. They offered the idol bread made with egg yolks, other pastries containing the hearts of deer, and another made with a paste of native pepper. There were many who drew blood, cutting their ears and anointing the stone they had there of the demon called *Chacacantun*. Here they would seize boys by force and draw blood from their ears by slashing them. They kept this statue and image until the fateful days were past, and meanwhile burned incense to them. When these days were gone, they carried the image to leave it in the North, and the statue to the temple. Then they went to their homes to attend to the preparations for the new year. If they did not do all these things, they could expect many eye ailments.

This year, in which the symbol *Muluc* was the Dominical letter and the *bacab Canzienal* reigned was held to be a good one because he, as they said, was the best and greatest of the *Bacabs*, and so they considered him first in their prayers. But despite all this, the evil spirit obliged them to make an idol called *Yaxcocahmut* and to place it in the temple, removing all the old images; to build in the court in front of the temple a stone pile on which to burn incense and a ball of the resin or milk called *kik*. There they payed to the idol and begged for protection against the bad times they feared for that year, which were shortage of water, many weak offshoots from maize plants, and things of this nature. Against this, the demon ordered them to offer him squirrels and a plain robe woven by the old women whose duty was to dance in the temple to please *Yaxcocahmut*.

Although this was a good year they had many other hardships and evil omens if they did not perfom the ceremonies that the demon instructed. This was to hold a festival where they were to do a dance on very high stilts and offer him the heads of turkeys, bread, and brinks made of maize. They were also to offer him clay dogs with bread on their backs, and the old women had to dance carrying these in their hands and sacrifice a little dog that had a black back and was virgin. The devout had to draw blood and with it anoint the stone of the demon *Chacacantun*. They regarded this sacrifice and ceremony was pleasing to their god *Yaxcocahmut*.

XXXVII

Sacrifices for the new year *Ix*. Evil omens and how to avert them.

In the year of which the Dominical letter was *Ix* and the patron Zaczini, after the election of a master to take charge of the celebrations, they would make a statue of the demon called *Zacuuayayab* and take it to the pile of stones in the North were they had left the image the year before. The made a statue of the demon Yzamná and stood it at the house of the master of ceremonies, then all together went devoutly along the decorated road for the image of *Zacuuayayab*. On arriving, they perfumed it with incense as they always did, cut off the head of a fowl and, putting the image on a pole called *Zachia*, bore it away with prayers and dances that they called alcabtan kamahau. The usual drink was brought out to the road for them, and when they reached the house of the patron they placed this image opposite the statue of *Yzamná*, where they all made their offerings and shared them out. To the statue of *Zacuuayayab* they offered the head of a turkey, pastries filled with quail or other things, and their drink.

Others drew blood and with it anointed the stone of the demon *Zacacantun*; and thus they attended the idols for the days that remained until the new year. They perfuned them with incense until the day after new year, when they took *Yzamná* to the temple and *Zacuuayayab* to the West, leaving it there ready to be fetched the following year.

The misfortunes they feared this year if they were careless in these ceremonies were fainting, collapse and eye ailments; they considered this year a disastrous one for bread, but good for cotton. This year, with the Dominical letter *Ix* which the *bacab Zaczini* governed, was held as an evil one because they said they would suffer many hardships in it, such a great drought and great heat that would scorch the maize fields. As a result there would be famine, and famine would be followed by theft, theft by the enslavement and sale of those who were guilty of it. From this would arise conflicts and wars amongst themselves or against other peoples. They also said that there would be changes in the ruls of the chiefs or priests because of the wars and disputes.

They also had a prophecy that some of those who would desire to become chiefs would not succeed. They said that locusts would come and that their towns would be laid waste by famine. What the demon ordered them to do to avert these misfortunes, some or all they believed would befall them, was to make an idol that they called *Chinchahau Izamná*. This they had to place in the temple, where they burned much incense, made many offerings and prayers and shed much blood, with which they amointed the stone of the demon *Zacacantun*. They performed many dances, and as was usual the old women danced. On this occassion they built a small new shrine to the demon, or renovated the old one, and there gathered to make sacrifices and offerings; and all got solemnly drunk, as this was a general and obligatory feast. There were some very devout people who, of their own will and theough devotion, made another idol like the one above and stood it in other temples, where offerings were made and heavy drinking took place. They held that drunkenness and sacrifices were most pleasing to the idols and were the way to free themselves of the disasters told by the prophecy.

XXXVIII

Sacrifices for the new year *Cauac*. Ill omens and how to avert them with the fire dance.

In the year when the Dominical letter was *Cauac* and the tutelary god *Horanek*, after having chosen a patron for the celebrations, they made in image of the demon *Ekuuayayab* and took it to the pile of stones in the West where they all went to the place where the image of *Ekuuayayab* stood, for which they had left the image the previous year.They also made a statue of the demon called *Uacmitunahau* and placed it at the house of the patron in a suitable spot. Then from there they had carefully prepared the road. On arrival, the priest and the chiefs burned incense to it as they always did and cut the head off a fowl. After this they took the image on a pole called *Yaxek*, putting on its back a skull and a corpse, and on top a carnivorous bird called *Kuch* [vulture] as a sign of a heavy death toll, since they held this year to be a very bad one.

Afterwards they carried it thus, with respect and devotion and performing some dances, one of which was like the *cazcarientas*, which they called *Xibalbaokot*, meaning 'the dance of the devil'. The stewards came out to the road with the drink of the chiefs, and this drink they took to the place of the statue of *Uacmitunahau* and put it in front of the image they carried. Then they began their offerings, incense-burning and prayers, and many drew blood from different parts of their bodies and with it anointed the stone of the demon called *Ekelacantun*. In this manner they passed the ill-omened days, at the end of which they took *Uacmitunahau* to the temple and *Ekuuayayab* to the South to fetch it the following year.

This year, in which the letter was *Cauac* and the *bacab Hozanek* governed they held to be disastrous in addition to the numerous deaths predicted, for they said that the fierce heat would wither the maize fields and the large number of ants and the birds would eat up whatever they sowed. But as this would not happen everywhere, in some places there would be food, though won with great difficulty. The demon would oblige them to mak four idols —*Chicacchob, Ekbolamchac, Ahcanuolcab* and *Ahbulucbalam*— to avert these evils and stand them in the temple where they perfumed them whith their incense, offered two balls of milky resin called *kik* to be burned, certain iguanas and bread, a miter-headdress and a bunch of flowers, and one of their precious stones. In addition to this, to celebrate the festival, they built a great vault of wood in the courtyard and piled firewood on top and at the sides, leaving openings through which to enter and leave. Wen this had been built, each of the other men took a handful of very dry sticks tied together, and with a singer standing on the top of the wood pyre who sang and beat a native drum, those below danced in perefect time and devotion, passing in and out through the openings in the wood vault. Thus they danced until evening, when leaving his bundle of rods there, each one went home to rest and eat.

At nightfall they returned, and with them a crowd of people, because this ceremony was held in great regard among them. Each one taking his torch, he lit it and one by one put it to the wood that burned fiercely and was rapidly consumed. When all was reduced to embers they leveled them out very smooth and those who had danced, and others, walked barefoot and naked as they were, across the ashes. Some crossed without harm, some were seriosly burned and others only slightly. The believed that in this lay the solution to their misfortunes and ill omens and thought that this was the most pleasing service to their gods. With this over, they went off to drink themselves drunk, as the custom of this festival and the heat of the fire demanded.

XXXIX

An explanation of the calendar

Using the Indian symbols shown above they gave names to the days of their months, and from all the months together made a sort of calendar. With this they regulated their festivals, accounts, trading and business, just as we do by our own calendar. But they did not begin their calendar with the first day of their year, but much later because of the complicated fashion they had of counting the days of their months all together, as will be seen from the calendar I shall give here. Because although the letters and days of their months are 20, their custom is to count them from 1 to 13. After 13 they began counting from 1 again, and thus divide the days of the year into 27 times 13, plus 11 days, without counting those of ill-omen.

With these jugglings and the cumbersome method it is a marvel to see the ease with which those who know it can count and understand. It is most remarkable that the Dominical letter always falls on the first day of their year without fail or error, and that no other day of the 20 ever appears in that position. They also used this method of counting to give another fashion of reckoning from those symbols that they used for ages and for other things that, although important to the Indians, do not concern us much here. Therefore, let them lie, with the observation that the character of letter with which they began their count of their days or calendar is called *Hun Imix*, which is this:

—which has no fixed or assigned day on which to fall because each symbol changes the count itself, and so the Dominical letter never fails to fall on the first day of the following year.

The first day of the year for these people was always the sixteenth of our month of July, and the first day of their months *Pop*. It is not to be wondered that these people, though simple in other things, we have found in this matter to possess the same care and good sense as other peoples have shown, for according to gloss on Ezekial, January was the beginning of the year for the Romans; for the Hebrews, April; for the Greeks, March, and October for the Eastern world. But although they begin their year in July, I shall put their calendar in no other order than ours, and together with ours, so that our letters will coincide with theirs, our months with theirs, and their count by thirteens compared to them, placed in numerical order.

Since there is no need to deal with the calendar in one place and the festivals in another, I shall include in each month the feasts, ceremonies and celebration with which they observed it. Thus I shall fulfill what I promised before: that I would set out their calendar and write of the fasts and ceremonies they observed when making their wooden idols and other things. All this, and the other things spoken of here, I intend only for the praise of almighty God, who has suffered this to exist and has seen fit to remedy in our times. And so, with deeply felt Christianity, we pray that these people may be preserved and find deliveramce in the true faith and that those charged with them may support and aid them so that for the sins of this people, or our own, they do not lack help; and that they may not fail in what has been begun and thus return to their misery and sins so that things worse than the original ones befall them, with the demons returning to dwell in their souls from where, with laborious care we have succeeded in expelling them cleansing and sweeping them clean of their vices and former evil habits. And it is not too much to fear this when we see the perdition that has existed for so many years all over great and most Christian Asia, in the good, Catholic and most august Africa, and the miseries and calamities that there are today in our own Europe. in our own country and in our homes. Thus we may say that the evangelical prophesies about Jerusalem —that her enemies would surround, weaken and pressure her so much that they would bring her to the ground— have been fulfilled. And God must have permitted this because of what we are, but his Church cannot fail, nor can what he said: *Nisi Dominus reliquisset semen, sicut Sodoma fuissemus.*

XL

The Roman and the Yucatecan calendars

JANUARY

Thirteens	Days	Months of the Indians		Thirteens	Days	Months of the Indians	
a	12	Ben		f	4	Ezanab	
b	13	Ix		g	5	Cauac	
c	1	Men		a	6	Ahau	
d	2	Cib		b	7	Imix	
e	3	Caban		c	8	Ik	
				d	9	Akbal	

According to the Indians, they set about creating gods with great respect. When the idols are finished and perfected, the owner of them made a gift, the best he was able to afford, of birds, game and their money, to pay for the work of those who had made the idols. They would take them out of the hut and stand them in another thatched shelter built for the purpose in the courtyard, where the priest blessed them with great solemnity and a large number of devout prayers. The priest and the artisans first cleaned themselves of soot, because they were said to fast while the idols were being made. Then, with the idol anointed and the evils spirit exorcised as usual and the sacred incense burned, they placed the idol, wrapped in a cloth, in a woven basket and presented it to the owner, who received it with great devoutness.

Then the good priest preached on the high merit of the occupation of making new gods and on the danger the makers risked in the event that they did not observe abstinence and fasts. Afterwards, they ate very well and drank even better.

e	10	Kan		c	2	Muluc	
f	11	Chicchan		d	3	Oc	
g	12	Cimi		e	4	Chuen	
a	13	Manik		f	5	Eb	
b	1	Lamat		g	6	Ben	
				a	7	Ix	

YAX   In either of the months *Chen* or *Yax*, on the day appointed by the priest, they held the festival that they called *Ocná*, which means "renovation of the temple". They celebrated this festival in honor of the *chacs* who were held to be gods of the corn fields and at it they examined the prognostications of the *bacabs*, as is explained at more length in its place in accordance with the order given. They celebrated this festival each year and at the same time replaced the clay idols and their braziers, as it was the custom for each idol to have a small brazier to burn incense in. If it was necessary, they built the house again or restored it and recorded the memory of these things on the wall in their characters.

b	8	Men		f	12	Cauac	
c	9	Cib		g	13	Ahau	

Here begins the calendar count of the Indians, called in their lenguage Hun Imix.

a	1	Imix	
b	2	Ik	
d	10	Caban	
c	3	Akbal	
e	11	Ezanab	

FEBRUARY

d	4	Kan		d	11	Chuen	
e	5	Chicchan		e	12	Eb	
f	6	Cimi		f	13	Ben	
g	7	Manik		g	1	Ix	
a	8	Lamat		a	2	Men	
b	9	Muluc		b	3	Cib	
c	10	Oc		c	4	Caban	

d	5	Ezanab		d	12	Chicchan	
e	6	Cauac		e	13	Cimi	
f	7	Ahau		f	1	Manik	
g	8	Imix		g	2	Lamat	
a	9	Ik		a	3	Muluc	
b	10	Akbal		b	4	Oc	
c	11	Kan		c	5	Chuen	

ZAC

On one day of this month *Zac*, decided by the priest, hunters held another celebration like the one in the month of *Zip* to placate the ire that the gods had against them and their sown fields. It was also to excuse themselves for the blood they had made flow on their hunts, because they held any shedding of blood in horror, save in their sacrifices, Because of this, whenever they went out hunting they prayed to their unholy god and burned incense to him, and if they could, they (later) smeared his face with blood from the heart to the victims of the chase.

Whatever day *7 Ahau* fell on they held a very great festival which lasted for three days, with incense, offerings and genteel drinking, and because this is a movable feast the priests were careful to announce it in sufficient time for people to fast properly.

CEH

MARCH

d	6	Eb		b	5	Kan
e	7	Bwn		c	6	Chicchan
f	8	Ix		d	7	Cimi
g	9	Men		e	8	Manik
a	10	Cib		f	9	Lamat
b	11	Caban		g	10	Muluc
c	12	Ezanab		a	11	Oc
d	13	Cauac		b	12	Chuen
e	1	Ahau		c	13	Eb
f	2	Imix		d	1	Ben
g	3	Ik		e	2	Ix
a	4	Akbal		f	3	Men

g	4	Cib		c	7	Cauac	
a	5	Caban		d	8	Ahau	
b	6	Ezanab		e	9	Imix	
				f	10	Ik	

MAC

On any day of this month of *Mac* the elderly and the oldest people held a celebration for the *chacs* the gods of food, and for *Itzamná*. One or two days before this they performed a curious ceremony which in their language they called *Tuppkak*. They sought out the animals and creatures there were in the countryside, and with them gathered on the temple courtyard where the *chacs* and the priest seated themselves in the corners as they were wont to do to exorcise the evil spirit, and each had a pitcher of water which was brought there to him. At the center they stood a bundle of dry sticks tied together Then, after burning their incense in a brazier they set fire to the sticks and as they burned they tore the hearts from the birds and animals and threw them on the fire to burn. If there were no large animals such as tigers, lions or alligators they made hearts of incense, but if there were these animals, and they killed them they brought their hearts for the fire. When all the hearts had burned, the *chacs* put the fire out with water from their pitchers. They celebrated this and the following ceremony to ensure a good year of rain for their maize. They celebrated the ceremony differently from the others, since they did not fast in preparation, except for the provider of the feast, who did. Come together to celebrate the festival the townspeople, priests and officials gathered in the temple court where they had made a pile of stones with stairways, all very clean and decorated with fresh foliage. The priest gave incense prepared by the provider, which was burned in a brazier and thus the evil spirit was said to be exorcised. Having done this with their usual devotion, they smeared the first step of the pile with mud from the well, and the rest of the steps with blue pitch. They burned a lot of incense and invoked the *chacs* and *Itzamná* with their prayers and rites and made their offerings. When this was over they comforted themselves by eating and drinking what had been offered, confident of a good year because of their prayers and invocations.

APRIL

g	11	Akbal	
a	12	Kan	
b	13	Chicchan	
c	1	Cimi	
d	2	Manik	
e	3	Lamat	
f	4	Muluc	
g	5	Oc	
a	6	Chuen	
b	7	Eb	
c	8	Ben	

KANKIN

d	9	Ix	
e	10	Men	
f	11	Cib	
g	12	Caban	
a	13	Ezanab	
b	1	Cauac	
c	2	Ahau	
d	3	Imix	
e	4	Ik	

f	5	Akbal		d	10	Lamat	
g	6	Kan		e	11	Muluc	
a	7	Chicchan		f	12	Oc	
b	8	Cimi		g	13	Chuen	
c	9	Manik		a	1	Eb	

MUAN

In the month of *Muan*, those who had cacao plantations held a festival for the gods *Ekchuah*, *Chac* and *Hobnil*, who were their mediators. They went to the property of one of them to carry the ceremony out, where they sacrificed a dog marked with the color of the cacao, burned incense to their idols and offered them iguanas of the blue species and the feathers of a certain bird and other game: then they gave each official a pod of cacao beans. When the sacrifice and their prayers were over they ate the gifts and supposedly drank three draughts of wine, no more, and went to the home of the man who was responsible for the fiesta and were happy to dance a few steps.

MAY

b	2	Ben		f	13	Kan
c	3	Ix		g	1	Chicchan
d	4	Men		a	2	Cimi
e	5	Cib		b	3	Manik
f	6	Caban		c	4	Lamat
g	7	Ezanab		d	5	Muluc
a	8	Cauac		e	6	Oc
b	9	Ahau		f	7	Chuen
c	10	Imix		g	8	Eb
d	11	Ik		a	9	Ben
e	12	Akbal		b	10	Ix
				c	11	Men

d	12	Cib		a	3	Ahau	
e	13	Caban		b	4	Imix	
f	1	Ezanab		c	5	Ik	
g	2	Cauac		d	6	Akbal	

PAX

In this month of *Pax* they held a celebration called *Pacumchac*, for which the chiefs and priests of the smaller settlements joined those of the larger towns and together they kept a vigil for five nights in the temple of *Citchaccoh*, with prayers, offerings and incense, as it is said they celebrate the fiesta of *Cuculcán*, *in the month of Xul*, in November. Before these days were over, they all went to the house of their war captain called the *Nacón* with whom I have dealt, and carried him with great pomp, perfuming him with incense like a temple idol, seated him and burned incense to him. There he and they stayed until the five days had elapsed, during which they ate and drank of the gifts that were offered in the temple and performed a dance in the manner of the slow stride of war and which they call *Holkanakot*, meaning dance of the warriors. After these five days they came to the fiesta which because it was for matters of war and victory over enemies, was very solemn. So first they performed the ceremony and sacrifices of the fire in the month of *Mac*, as I said; then they cast out the evil spirit with great solemnity as they do, and when this has been done then came prayers and the offering of gifts and incense. While the people were making their offerings, the chiefs took the *Nacón* on their shoulders and carried him around the temple, burning incense. When they returned with him, the *chacs* would sacrifice a dog, remove its heart and give it to the demon between two plates. The *chacs* each broke large pots full of drink, and with this they ended their fiesta. Once over, they ate and drank the gifts which had been offered there and took the *Nacón* back to this house with great solemnity but without perfume.

There they held a great feast at which the chiefs, the priests and the leading men drank themselves drunk and the rest of the people returned to their villages, but the *Nacón*, did not get drunk.The next day, when the alcohol had been well digested, all the village chiefs and priests who had become intoxicated and stayed there gathered in the house of the chief, who distributed great quantities of incense that he had there ready and blessed by their unholy priests. As well as this, he made a speech and strongly commended them the ceremonies that they should hold in their own villlages for the year to be productive in food. After this speech they all took leave of one another with noisy expressions of affection and each one went away to his village.

There they busied themselves in their celebrations which, depending on how they were organized, lasted until the month of *Pop*. These were called *Zabcilthan*, and were thus: first they looked about in the town, among the richest, for someone who would give the feast and set the day for it so as to have the greatest pleasure during the three months until their new year. What they did was to assemble in the house of the man who provided the feast and there perform the ceremonies of exorcising the evil spirit, burn incense and make offerings with merry-making and dances and making themselves into wineskins, and that is how it went on. And there was so much excess during these three monts of celebrations that it was pitiful to see them, as some went about scratched, some with broken heads, and others with their eyes bloodshot from drinking so much.But despite all this, they were so fond of wine that they gave themselves over to it.

JUNE

e	7	Kan	
f	8	Chicchan	
g	9	Cimi	
a	10	Manik	
b	11	Lamat	
c	12	Muluc	
d	13	Oc	
e	1	Chuen	
f	2	Eb	
g	3	Ben	
a	4	Ix	
b	5	Men	
c	6	Cib	

KAYAB

d	7	Caban	
e	8	Ezanab	
f	9	Cauac	
g	10	Ahau	
a	11	Imix	
b	12	Ik	
c	13	Akbal	
d	1	Kan	

CUMKU

e	2	Chicchan	
f	3	Cimi	
g	4	Manik	

a	5	Lamat			d	8	Chuen	
a	6	Muluc			e	9	Eb	
e	7	Oc			f	10	Ben	

JULY

g	11	Ix	
a	12	Men	
b	13	Cib	
c	1	Caban	
d	2	Ezanab	
e	3	Cauac	
f	4	Ahau	
g	5	Imix	

a	6	Ik	
b	7	Akbal	
c		Kan	
d		Chicchan	
e		Cimi	
f		Manik	
g		Lamat	

It has been told in earlier chapters how the Indian began their years after the unnamed days, preparing themselves during these days, like during Lent, for the celebration of their New Year festival. In addition to the preparation they made by performing the ceremony of the god *Uuayayab*, for which they let their houses, the other preparations were to leave their houses very little during these five days and to offer, besides gifts for the general festival, beads to their own gods and to the others in their temples. These beads that they offered thus they never took for their own use, nor anything else that they offered to the demon, but they used to buy incense for burning. During these days they neither combed their hair nor washed; neither men nor women killed their lice and did nothing humble or difficult, because they feared that some evil would befall them if they did.

a	12	Kan		b	7	Eb	
a	13	Chicchan		c	8	Ben	
c	1	Cimi		d	9	Ix	
d	2	Manik		e	10	Men	
e	3	Lamat		f	11	Cib	
f	4	Muluc		g	12	Caban	
g	5	Oc		a	13	Ezanab	
a	6	Chuen		b	1	Cauac	

POP   The first day of *Pop* is the first day of the first month of
the Indians; it was their New Year, and a great festival
among them because it was general and for all. Thus, all
the town together feted all the idols. To celebrate more
solemnly, on this day they replaced all their household articles, such
as plates, vessels, benches, old clothes and the wraps in which they
kept their idols. They swept out their houses, throwing rubbish and
old useless items onto a midden outside the village, and no one touched
them, even if having need of them. For this festival, the priest and the
leading men and those who so wished out of devoutness began to fast
and have no relations with their wives for a certain time beforehand,
according to what they considered right. Some began their abstinence
three months before, some two months, and others as they saw fit, but
no-one for less than thirteen days. In these thirteen days, as well as
abstaining from their wives, they did not eat either salt or hot peppers
in their food, which was held among them to be a great act of penance.
At this time they chose the *chacs*, officials to assist the priest, who prepared many pellets of fresh incense in some small molds that priests
had, and this same incense was burned to the idols by those who had
observed abstinence and fasted. Those who began these fasts would
not dare to break them for they believed that this would bring some
evil upon themselves or their households.

AUGUST

c   2   Ahau

d   3   Imix

e   4   Ik

f   5   Akbal

g   6   Kan

UO

a   7   Chicchan

b   8   Cimi

c   9   Manik

   With the arrival of the New Year, all the men assembled, alone, in the temple courtyard, because no women were allowed to be present at any sacrifice or ceremony performed in the temple, save the old women who were to do their dances. Women could go and attend ceremonies that were held in other places. The men came all clean and elegantly painted with their red unguents and washed of the black soot that they smeared themselves with when they were fasting. Wen all were assembled, together with many gifts of food and drink, and much wine they had made, the priest purified the temple, seating himself in the middle of the courtyard in his ceremonial robes with a small brazier and the incense molds near him. The *chacs* took their seats in the four corners and stretched a new rope from one to the other to form a square which all those who had fasted had to enter in order to exorcise the evil spirit. With the evil spirit driven out, they all began to say their devout prayers and the *chacs* made the new fire. They burned incense to their evil god and the priest began to throw his incense onto the brazier; and they all approached in order, beginning with the chiefs, to receive incense from the hand of the priest. This he handed to them with all the sedateness and devotion as if he were giving them holy relics, and they threw it little by little onto the brazier, waiting until it had finished burning.

   After the burning of incense they all ate the offerings and gifts, and wine flowed until they were completely intoxicated. This was their New Year and a ritual most pleasing to their idols. Afterwards there were some who out of devoutness celebrated this festival of the month of *Pop* with their friends, the chiefs and the priests, for the priests were always the most important figures in their feasting and drinking.

d	10	Lamat		a	1	Eb	
e	11	Muluc		b	2	Ben	
f	12	Oc		c	3	Ix	
g	13	Chuen		d	4	Men	

e	5	Cib	
f	6	Caban	
g	7	Ezanab	
a	8	Cauac	
b	9	Ahau	
c	10	Imix	
d	11	Ik	
e	12	Akbal	

f	13	Kan	
		ZIP	
g	1	Chicchan	
a	2	Cimi	
b	3	Manik	
c	4	Lamat	
d	5	Muluc	
e	6	Oc	

In the month of *Uo* the priests, doctors and sorcerers —who were all the same— began to prepare themselves for the festival with fasting and all the other things. Hunters and fishermen came to celebrate this on the seventh day of *Zip*, each group separately and on their own day. First were the priests, whose feast was called Pocam. They gathered in all their finery in the house of the chief and first expelled the evil spirit as was the custom. then took out their books and laid them out on the foliage they had made ready for the purpose. Invoking with their prayers and devotion an idol called *Cinchau-Izamná*, who they said was the first priest, they offered him their gifts and burned pellets of incense on a new fire. Meanwhile, in a vessel they dissolved a little verdigris in virgin water, as they called it, brought from the forest where no woman ever went, and with this anointed the wooden covers of the books to purify them. This done, the most learned of the priests would open a book and look at the predictions for that year. He then announced them to those present and preached to them a little, prescribing the correct observances. Also at this ceremony he designated the priest or chief who was to be responsible for it the coming year and if the one he appointed for this died his sons were under the obligation to fulfill the charge on behalf of the deceased. When this had been done they ate all the gifts and food that they had brought, and drank until they were inebriated, and thus ended the ceremony, during which they sometimes performed a dance called *Okotuil*.

SEPTEMBER

f	7	Chuen		a	3	Ahau	
g	8	Eb		b	4	Imix	
a	9	Ben		c	5	Ik	
b	10	Ix		d	6	Akbal	
c	11	Men		e	7	Kan	
d	12	Cib		f	8	Chicchan	
e	13	Caban		g	9	Cimi	
f	1	Ezanab		a	10	Manik	
g	2	Cauac		b	11	Lamat	

c	12	Muluc		b	5	Men
d	13	Oc		c	6	Cib
e	1	Chuen		d	7	Caban
f	2	Eb		e	8	Ezanab
g	3	Ben		f	9	Cauac
a	4	Ix		g	10	Ahau

The following day, the physicians and sorcerers assembled in the house of one of them, together with their wives, and the priests expelled the evil spirit; this done, they unwrapped their medicines, where they had many trifles and each a little idol of the goddess of medicine named *Ixchel*, for which this ceremony is named *Ihcil Ixchel*. And they also had some stones for casting fortunes that were called *Am*. Then with great devotion they invoked their gods of medicine with prayers, and these were *Izamná*, *Citbolontun* and *Ahau Chimahez*. The priests offered them incense, which they burned on the brazier burning with the new fire. Meanwhile, the *chacs* smeared these things with another blue paste like that of the books of the priests. When this was done, each one wrapped up the tools of his trade and, taking the bundle on his back, they all performed a dance called *Chan-tun-yab*. After the dance, the men seated themselves together in one place and the women in another, and after drawing lots for the feast the following year, they ate the gifts and drank themselves senseless, except the priests who, they say, had some decency and kept the wine to drink alone and at their leisure.

On the following day the hunters gathered in the house of one of their number, bringing their wives like the others; then the priests came and expelled the evil spirit as usual. After this, they placed in the center the necessary articles for the sacrifice of incense and new fire, and the blue paste. Then the hunters invoked with prayers the gods of the hunt, *Acanum, Zuhuyzib, Zipitabai*, and others, they were given incense which trey threw onto the brazier. And while this was burning, each one produced an arrow and the skull of a deer, which the *chacs* anointed with the blue paste, and holding them thus anointed in their hands, they danced. Some pierced their ears, and others their tongues, and through the holes passed seven quite broad leaves of a plant they call *Ac*. After first doing this, the priest and the officers of the feast then offered their gifts and, as they danced, wine was served and they drank until completely intoxicated.

The following day the fishermen held their ceremony in the same way as the others, except that what was anointed was their fishing tackle, and they did not pierce their ears but rather tore the edges, and did their own dance called *Chohom*. After all this they blessed a tall, thick pole and set it upright. Their custom was, after the ceremony had been performed in the villages, for the chiefs and many people to go and celebrated it on the coast. There they spent their time fishing a great deal and enjoying themselves, having taken a large supply of nets, hooks and other equipment they use for fiishing. The patron gods of this festival were *Ahkaknexoi, Ahpua* and *Ahcitzamalcun*.

ZODZ

In the month of *Zodz* bee-keepers prepared themselves to celebrate their festival in *Tzec*, and although the chief preparation for these celebrations was fasting, only the priest and his assistants were under this obligation; for the others it was voluntary.

OCTOBER

a	11	Imix		g	11	Ix	
b	12	Ik		a	12	Men	
c	13	Akbal		b	13	Cib	
d	1	Kan		c	1	Caban	
e	2	Chicchan		d	2	Ezanab	
f	3	Cimi		e	3	Cauac	
g	4	Manik		f	4	Ahau	
a	5	Lamat		g	5	Imix	
b	6	Muluc		a	6	Ik	
c	7	Oc		b	7	Akbal	
d	8	Chuen		c	8	Kan	
e	9	Eb		d	9	Chicchan	
f	10	Ben		e	10	Cimi	

f 11 Manik

b 1 Oc

g 12 Lamat

c 2 Chuen

a 13 Muluc

TZEC   When the day of the festival came, they got themselves ready in the house where it was to be held and did all that was done in other ceremonies, save letting blood. Their patrons were the *bacabs*, especially *Hobnil*. They made many offerings, and in particular gave to the four *chacs* four plates with balls of incense in the middle of each one and the rims painted with figures in honey, because the ceremony was for the abundance of the same. They ended this with wine, as customary, because the owners of hives contributed large amounts of honey for it.

XUL   The departure of *Cuculcán* from Yucatán has already been related, and after this there were some among the Indians who said that he had gone to heaven with the gods. Therefore, they held him as a god and gave him a temple where his feast as such could be celebrated, and this was observed in all the country until the destruction of *Mayapán*. After this, the feast was held only in the province of *Mani*, while the other provinces, in recognition of what they owed to *Cuculcán* presented *Mani* one in one year and one in another, or in their turn, five magnificent feather banners with which they celebrated the festival in the following manner, and not like the others.

On the sixteenth day of *Xul* all the chiefs and priests gathered together in *Mani* and with them great numbers of people from the villages, who came prepared with fasting and abstinences. In the evening of that day they set forth from the house of the chief where they had assembled, together with a great company of people and many of their farce players, and and walked in solemn silence to the temple of *Cuculcán*, which was all decorated in readiness. On arrival, they said their prayers, stood the banners on the top of the temple and below, in the forecourt they all laid each one of their idols on leaves of trees there for that purpose. After kindling the new fire, they began to burn in-

NOVEMBER

d	3	Eb		b	2	Kan	
e	4	Ben		c	3	Chicchan	
f	5	Ix		d	4	Cimi	
g	6	Men		e	5	Manik	
a	7	Cib		f	6	Lamat	
b	8	Caban		g	7	Muluc	
c	9	Ezanab		a	8	Oc	
d	10	Cauac		b	9	Chuen	
e	11	Ahau		c	10	Eb	
f	12	Imix		d	11	Ben	
g	13	Ik		e	12	Ix	
a	1	Akbal		f	13	Men	

g	1	Cib		c	4	Cauac	
a	2	Caban		d	5	Ahau	
b	3	Ezanab		e	6	Imix	

cense in many places and to make offerings of dishes cooked without salt or hot peppers, and of their drink made of beans and pumpkin seeds. Burning incense all the time, the chiefs did not return to their houses, nor did those who had helped them, spending five days and five nights in prayer and in sacred dances. Until the first day of *Yxkin*, the players went about during these five days in the principal houses giving pantomimes and collecting the gifts they were offered, all of which they took to the temple. After these five days were over, the gifts were distributed among the chiefs, priests and dancers, the banners and idols were taken up, and they all returned to the house of the chief, and from there each one to his own. They said, and firmly believed, that on the final day *Cuculcán* descended from heaven and received this cremonies, abstinences and offerings. They call this festival *Chickabán*.

YAXKIN   In this month of *Yaxkin* they would as usual begin to make ready for the general festival they celebrated in *Mol* on the day appointed by the priest, for all the gods. They called it *Olob-Zab-Kamyax*. What they would do, after gathering in the temple and performing the ceremonies and burning incense as in the previous festivals, was to anoint all the tools of all the trades and offices with the blue paste they made, from those of the priest to the spindles of the women and the posts of their houses. For this festival they gathered together all the young boys and girls of the village and, instead of painting and ceremonies, they gave each one a few light blows on the knuckles. For the girls, this was done by and old woman dressed in a robe of feathers, who had brought them there and for this reason was called *Ixmol*, meaning 'the gatherer'. They were given these blows so that they would grow up to be skilled in the occupations of their mothers and fathers. The conclusion was a fine

DECEMBER

f	7	Ik		e	7	Men	
g	8	Akbal		f	8	Cib	
a	9	Kan		g	9	Caban	
b	10	Chicchan		a	10	Ezanab	
c	11	Cimi		b	11	Cauac	
d	12	Manik		c	12	Ahau	
e	13	Lamat		d	13	Imix	
f	1	Muluc		e	1	Ik	
g	2	Oc		f	2	Akbal	
a	3	Chuen		g	3	Kan	
b	4	Eb				CHEN	
c	5	Ben					
d	6	Ix		a	4	Chicchan	

b	5	Cimi		f	9	Oc
c	6	Manik		g	10	Chuen
d	7	Lamat		a	11	Eb
e	8	Muluc				

carouse, once the offerings had been eaten, except that it is possible that the devout old woman would take something home on which to get drunk so as not to lose the feathers of her robe of office on the way.

MOL

In this month, the beekeepers celebrated another festival like the one in the month of *Tzec*, so that the gods would provide flowers for the bees.

One of the things that these poor people held as most difficult and laborious was the making of wooden idols, which they called making gods. They had a special time appointed for making them, and this was the month of *Mol*, or another one if the priest told them it was fitting. Those who wished to make them first consulted the priest, and on his advice, then went to the maker of idols. They say that these artisans always tried to refuse, because they feared that they themselves or some member of their household would be sure to die, or be stricken with a fatal sickness. If they agreed however, the *chacs*, who were also chosen for this, began their fasts. While they fasted, the one who was having the idols made went himself, or sent someone, into the forest for the wood, which was always cedar. When the wood arrived they built a small hut of thatch, fenced off, where they put it and a large earthern jar in which to place the idols and keep them covered up while they were making them. They also took in incense to burn to four gods called *Acantuns*, which were placed at the four cardinal points. They also had in the hut things with which to cut themselves or draw blood from their ears, and the tools for carving their vile gods. When all had been made ready, the *chacs*, the priest and the sculptor shut themselves in the hut and began their work of making gods, cutting their ears frequently and anointing those demons with the blood, and burning incense to them. And so they continued until they finished, then they were given food. They were forbidden to have relations with their wives, even in thought, and no-one was allowed to approach the place where they were.

XLI

The century of the Mayas. Their writing

Not only did the Indians keep account of the years and months, as has been stated and described earlier, but they also had a certain way of counting time and their affairs by ages. These went twenty years by twenty years, and they counted thirteen thimes with each of the 20 symbols of the days that they called *Ahau*, not in order, but backwards, as they appear in the following circle on the following page.

They call these periods *Katun* in their language, and with them kept the reckoning of their ages wonderfully well, and so it was easy for the old man I mentioned in the first chapter to call to mind events that had happened three hundred years earlier. If I did not know about these reckonings of theirs I would not believe it possible for anyone to remember so much time.

As to who it was who invented this count of *Katuns*, if it was the devil he did what the usually does, drawing it up in his honor; if it was a man, he must have been most idolatrous, because he added to these *Katuns* all the chief deceptions, omens and fallacies by which these people went about completely deluded, in addition to all their other miseries. This was the lore in which they most believed, most respected, and which not all the priests could explain. The way they had for keeping account of their affairs and making divinations by this system was to have two idols in the temple dedicated to two of these symbols. To the first, beginning with the cross shown on the circle above, they offered prayers, ceremonies and sacrifices to avert the disasters of their 20 years, and in the last ten years of the twenty, they only burned incense to the idol and did reverence to it.

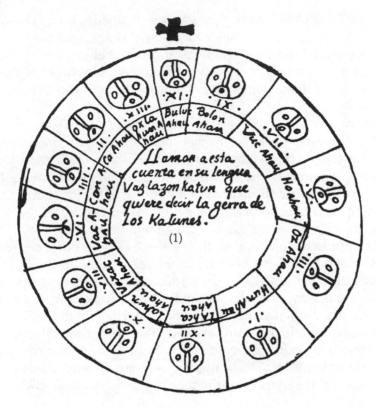

1 They call this count Vazlazon katun in their language which means
the war of the katuns.

After the twenty years of the first one, they began to be guided by
the fates of the second and, removing that first idol, set up another to
venerate it for the next ten years.

For example: The Indians say that the Spaniards finally reached the
city of Mérida in the year of our Lord 1541, which was exactly the first
year of the age of *Buluc-Ahau*, which is in the section where the cross
stands, and they arrived in the same month of *Pop*, which is the first
month of their year. But for the Spanish they would have worshiped
the idol *Buluc-Ahau* until the year '51, or for ten years, and in the tenth
year would have set up another idol, *Bolon-Ahau* to worship, guided
by his prophesies until the year '61, Then they would have taken it
from the temple and se up the idol of *Uuc. Ahau* and followed the pre-

dictions of *Bolon-Ahau*; thus they gave each one its turn. Thus, they venerated these *Katuns* of theirs for twenty years, and for ten years were governed by their superstitions and false beliefs, which were so many and quite enough to deceive simple people who hold them in awe though not those who know of natural matters and of the devil's skill in using them.

These people also used certain characters or letters to record their ancient history and their lore in their books; and with these symbols and some marks on them they recorded their affairs, made them known and taught. We found a great number of books written in these letters of theirs and, because they contained nothing in which there was not superstition and falsehoods of the devil, we burned all of them. This the Indians felt very deeply and it gave them great grief.

I shall put here an a, b, c, of their letters, as their cumbersome nature does not admit more, because they use them for all the sounds of the letters in a character, and then add part of another, going on *ad infinitum* in this way, as can be seen in the following example. *Le* means 'lasso' and 'to hunt with a lasso'. In order to write *le* in their characters, though we had made them understand that there are two letters, they wrote using three, putting the vowel *e* in front of the sound of the lleter *l*, which it has before it, and in this they are not wrong, although they use another *e*, if they wish, for the sake of precision. Example:

e   l   e   lé

afterwards, at the end, they put the syllables joined together.

Ha, which means 'water', because the name of the letter *aitch*, has an *a* sound at the beginning, they write with *a* before and finally in this manner:

They can also write in syllables, but in first one and then another way, which I woud not put here except to give a complete account of the customs of these people. *Ma in Kati* means 'I do not wish', and they write it in parts thus:

a   ha

ma   i   n   ka   ti

This is their a, b, c:

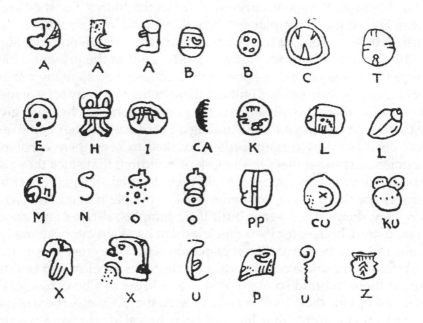

The letters that do not appear here are lacking in this language, but there are others in addition to ours for other sounds. Nowadays they do not use their own characters at all, particularly younger people, who have learned ours.

XLII

The multitude of buildings in Yucatán. Those of Izamal, Mérida and Chichén Itzá.

If Yucatán were to have won name and reputation for the great number, grandeur and beauty of its buildings as other parts of the Indies have done by reason of gold, silver and riches, its fame would have spread like that of Peru and New Spain, for so rich is it in buildings;

and there is such a great number of them that they are the most remarkable of all things discovered so far in the Indies. For they are so
many, and so many the places where they stand, and they are so well
built of dressed stone, in their own fashion, that it is a wonderful sight.
And because this country, though good, is not at the present what it
seems to have been in those prosperous times when so many remarkable buildings were erected without there being there any type of metal
for working them, I shall here put the explanations I have heard given
by those who have seen these buildings. These are that the people must
have been ruled by certain lords who liked to keep them constantly
occupied and so set them to the task of building; that since they used
to be suh devout worshipers of idols, they decided all together to build
temples for them. Later, for some reason, people moved, and wherever they then settled again built their temples, shrines and, as was
their custom, houses for their chiefs, which have always been made of
wood and thatched. Another explanation is that the great supply there
is of stone, lime and a certain white earth that is excellent for building
caused them to build so many that it would seem a hoax to speak of
them, except for the people who have seen them. Or else there is some
secret to this country that has not been revealed to the native until
now, and has not passed down to these times. To say that these buildings were constructed by other nations that put pressure on the Indians is not true, because there are signs that they were built by the naked Indians themselves. This can be seen in one of the many large buildings that still stand, from the walls of the bastions, where there are still
traces of men, naked except for having their parts covered with some
long strips of cloth that they call *Ex* in their language, and with others
articles that the Indians wear today. These are fashioned in very hard
mortar.

While I was living there, a large jar with three handles, painted on
the outside with some silvery stripes was found in a building we pulled
down. Inside this were the ashes of a cremated body, and among these
we found three complete stone beads of the type the Indians now use
as coin, all of which shows that the Indians were the builders. However, if indeed they were, they were of more stuff than those of now,
and much better in body and strength. This can be seen better in Izamal
than elsewhere, from the semi-relief cement figures that, as I have said,
still exist on the bastions, which are of well-grown men. The extremi-

ties of the arms and legs, of which were the ashes in the urn we found in the buildding, were very large and curiously unburned.

There is here at Izamal one building among the others that is amazingly tall and handsome, which can be seen in the drawing and is the reason for it. It was twenty steps, each more than two good handspans in height and width, and they must be over one hundred feet long. These steps are made of very large dressed stones but now, because of time and being exposed to the rain, they are worn and damaged. Around them is a very strong wall of cut stone, as shown by the curved line on which, at about one and a half times the height of a man there is

(1) capilla
(2) escalera
(3) descanso o plaça
(4) Plaça muy grande, y hermosa.
(5) Escaleros muy agras de subir

1. Chapel. 2 Stairway. 3 Landing or plaza. 4 Very large and beautiful plaza. 5. Stairs very difficult to climb.

a cornice of fine stones that runs all the way around. From this, the building rises until it is level tiwh the platform that extends from the top step. At the back of the platorm is another staircase like the first, although not so broad nor with so many steps, with the wall still encircling it. At the top of these steps is another fine court and there, quite close to the wall, stands a very high mound with its stairway on the south side, like the other great stairs. On top is a handsome chapel built of finely worked stone. I climbed to the top of this chapel and, since Yucatán is a flat country, from there I had a magnificent view of the land as far as the eye can reach, as far as the sea. There used to be eleven or twelve of these buildings in all at Izamal, but this one is the largest, and they were all near one another. No-one remembers who the builders were, but they seem to have been the first inhabitants. The buildings are eight leagues from the sea on a fine site on good, well populated land. For this reason, in 1549 the Indians pressed us to found a monastery in one of the buildings, which we call San Antonio. Here and in all the surrounding district great assistance has been given to them in the matter of their Christianity, and thus two fine communities, separate from each other, have been established in this area.

The second most important buildings in this country –and so ancient that there is no record of their builders– are those of *T-ho*; these lie thirteen leagues from those of Izamal and, like these, eight leagues away from the sea. There are still signs today of there having once been a fine avenue running from one lot of buildings to the other. The Spanish founded a city here calling it Mérida because of the curiosity and grandeur of its buildings. The principal ones I shall here describe as ably as I can, as I did for the one at Izamal, so that it may be better seen as it was.

This is the drawing I was able to make of the building, and so as to understand it, account must be taken of the fact that this is a ruined site of great size, more than two runs of a horse along each side. The stairway rises on the east front, being of seven steps as high as those of Izamal. The other sides, in the south, west and north, rise from a very strong, thick wall. All the base of the square is made of dry stone, and on the flat part another staircase begins in the east that is in my judgment some 28 to 30 feet long and set back from other stairs just as large. It is likewise set back on the north and south sides, but not in the west, After this there are two strong walls that run until they meet or join those of the court on the west side and so reach to the mass of the staircase. And all this makes up the central bulk of dry stone, and the grandeur of such a pile built by hand is wonderful to see.

Then, on the top level, the buildings begin thus: on the east side, set back some six feet, is a wing that so does not reach the ends. Built of fine stone carved on both sides it is made up of cells twelve feet long

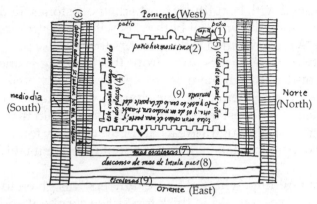

1. Chapel. 2. Very beautiful plaza. 3. Landing reached by this stairway. 4. This room is long divided into two plazas. 5. Cells on each side. 6. These were cells on one side and the other and the one in the center was a passageway and so was the one in the west. 7. More steps. 8. Platform of more than 30 feet. 9. Steps.

Building at T-ho after the sketch in Landa's account

by eight feet wide. The doorways in the center of each of them have no sign of jambs or any type of pivots that would allow them to be closed but are plain, of finely worked stone. It is all wonderfully built, and all the doorways are capped with single blocks of stone. In the center is an a passage arched like a bridge, and above the entrances to the cells is a projecting relief of carved stone that runs all along the wing. From this there rose some small pillars to the top, hald of them rounded and carved, and half engaged in the wall. These pillars reached to the top of the vaults that roofed and covered the chambers. Above these pillars there was another relief that ran around the whole wing. The ceilings were flat and made of a very hard stucco that they make with water prepared from the bark of a special tree. On the north side there was another series of small chambers just like the others, but it was only about half as long. The chambers continued on the west side, and every four or five there was a vault across like the one in the center of the east part. There was then there was a round building, quite large, and then another arch, and the rest was chambers like the others. This wing crosses most of the large platform and so forms two courts, one at the back in the west, and the other in the east. The last of these is very different because it faces south and has two chambers closed with a vault. The first part of these chambers has a corridor with very thick columns capped with beautifully worked whole stones. In the middle is a wall on which the vault of both rests with two entrances into the other room. A whitewashed ceiling covers the whole.

About two stone throws away from this building is another very high, fine court in which there are three piles of very well hewn masonry, and on top of them their fine chapels with vaults, as they usually built them. Some distance away there is a pyramid that is so wonderfully large that, although a great part of the city they founded around it was built with stones taken from it, I doubt whether it will ever come to an end.

The first building, with the four chambers was given to us by the governor Montejo, covered in thick forest; we cleared it and on it, using its own stones, we built a porper monastery all of stone, and a fine church that we named Mother of God. There was so much stone from the chambers that the one in the south and in part those of the sides are still entire, though we gave much stone to the Spanish settlers for their houses, especially for doors and windows; such was the great quantity.

The buildings at the town of Tikoch are neither so many nor so splendid as some of the others, though they were good and worthy. I would not mention them here, save because there must have been a large population in the town, which must of necessity be spoken of further on, and therefore I shall no say more here. These buildings are three leagues east of *Izamal*, and seven from *Chicheniza*.

Chicheniza, then, is splendid site ten leagues from *Izamal* and eleven from Valladolid. According to old Indians, here ruled three lords, brothers who, as they recalled having heard from their forefathers, came to that land from the west. Here they brought together a great town of many peoples and tribes that they ruled for several years in full peace and justice.

The revered their gods highly and therefore raised many beautiful buildings to them, in particular one, the largest, of which I shall give the design as I drew when I was there on it, so that it may be better understood.

These lords, they say, lived most uprightly without women, and all the time they lived thus they were highly respected and obeyed by all. Then, as time went by, one of them disappeared —he must have died, but the Indians say that he left the country through *Bac halal*. His

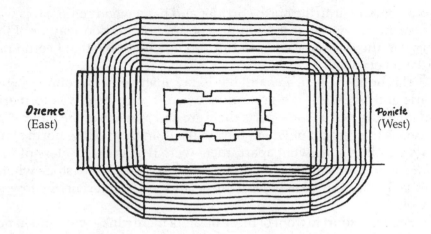

Oriente
(East)

Poniete
(West)

absence, however it came about, affected those who ruled after him so much that they then began to show favoritism in the realm and to become so immodest and dissolute in their ways that the people came to hate them. Such was their hate that they killed them, dismantling and abandoning the site, leaving behind the buildings and this site that is so beautiful because it is near the sea, only ten leagues distant, with very fertile lands and areas surrounding it. The design of the main building is as follows.

This structure has four staircases placed at the four cardinal points, each one 32 feet wide and with 91 steps that are laborious to climb. The steps have the same rise and width as we give to ours. Each staircase has two low ramps level with the steps, two feet wide and made of well-dressed stone, like all the building. The structure has no sharp corners, because from the ground up as far as the ramps there are some round-cut blocks that rise by stages and the building thus tapers very gracefully.

When I saw it there was a creature with a serpent's jaws at the foot of each ramp, very skillfully carved from a single block of stone. The stairways ended thus, and at the top there is a small flat platform where stands a building made of four chambers. Three of these run round without interruption; each one has doorways halfway along and is roofed with a vault. The north chamber is separated by a corridor of thick pullars. The chamber in the center, which must have been a sort of small court formed by the placement of the walls of the building, has a doorway into the north corridor and has a wood ceiling; this was where incense was burned. On the entrance of this doorway, or of the corridor, there is some sort of arms carved on a stone that I could not discern very well.

This building had, and still has today, many others around it, well made and large. All the ground between it and them was formerly paved white and in some parts there are still remains of the paving, so strong is the cement of which they make it. In front of the north stairway, standing somewhat apart, there were two small theaters of masonry, with four staircases and paved on top with slabs of stone where, it is said, farces and comedies were performed to entertain the townspeople.

From the court in front of these theaters there runs a wide and handsome paved causeway leading to a well about three stone throws away. Into this well they had had the custom, and still had at that time, of throwing living men as sacrifices to the gods in times of drought. The believed that they did not die, even though they were never seen again. They also threw in many precious stones and other things they valued, so, if there had been gold in this country, this well would contain most of it, seeing how much the Indians revered it. The well is seven long fathoms deep to the surface of the water, more than one hundred feet across, round, and the rock is wonderfully sheer down to the water. It seems to have very green water in it, and I think this is caused by the woods that surround it; it is very deep. At the top, near the mouth, stands a small building where I found idols made in honor of all the chief gods of the country, almost like the Pantheon at Rome. I do not know whether this was an ancient invention or one of the modern ones, so as to find their idols when they came to the well with offerings. I found such statues of lions, pitchers and other things that I do not know how anyone can say that these people had no metal tools. I also found two men of great stature, each carved out of a single block of stone, naked, but their private parts covered in the way the Indians covered themselves. The heads were separate pieces, with rings in their ears like those the Indians used, and a tang at the back of the head that fitted into a deep hole in the neck made for it, which so completed the statue.

XLIII

For what things the Indians made other sacrifices

The festivals in the calendar of these people that are described earlier show us what and how many they were, and how and why they were celebrated. But because these festivals were only to keep their gods content and benevolent, when they were held to be angry, they made them more bloody. They believed that the gods were angry when suffering from want, pests, dissentions, unfruitfulnes of crops, or similar misfortunes. In these cases they did not try to appease the demon gods by sacrificing animals or making them solemn offerings of food and drink or by shedding their blood and inflicting on themselves vigils, fasts and abstinence. Rather, forgetting all natural mercy and reason, they made sacrifices to them of human beings, with as much unconcern as if they were sacrificing birds, and as often as the accursed priests or the *chilanes* told them was necessary, or as the chiefs fancied or felt desirable. And since there were not so many people in this country as in Mexico, and after the fall of Mayapán they were ruled not by one chief but by many, they did not slaughter so many people all together. Nevertheless, many did not fail to die miserably, since each town had the power to sacrifice however many the priest, *chilán* or chief thought fit; and for this they had public places in their temples as if it were the most necessary thing in the world for the preservation of the state. Besides killing in the towns, they had those unholy sanctuaries of *Chichenizá* and *Cuzmil*, where they sent innumerable wretches to be sacrificed, or to be hurled down, another to have his heart ripped from him. May the merciful Lord, who saw fit to sacrifice himself on the cross to the Father of all men consent to preserve us from such miserable errors for ever.

O Lord my God, being, light and life of my soul, holy guide and sure path in my daily course, solace in my grief, inner joy of my suffering, comfort and rest within my labors. Why dost thou order me what may be called your work and not much preferably rest? Why dost thou try me with rasks that I cannot fittingly perform? Lord, dost thou perchance not know the measure of thy vassel, the strength of my limbs and the nature of my forces? Dost thou, Lord, desert me in my labors?

Art thou not the loving Father of whom the prophet spoke thus in the psalm saying: "I am with him in the midst of tribulations and trials, and I shall deliver him from them and bring him to glory"?

Lord thou art, and thou art He of whom the prophet filled with thy most Holy Spirit spoke thus, saying that thou maketh a burden of thy command; and thus it is, Lord, that those who have not enjoyed the sweetness of keeping and fulfilling thy commands find them burdensome; but, Lord, it is a false burden, a feared task, a burden to the weak in spirit, feared by those men who never decide to put their hands to the plow so as to accomplish it. Those who are willing to obey thy commands find them sweet and seek the odor of thy salves; their sweetness comforts them at every step, and they find much more pleasure every day —who no-one else can see— like another queen of Saba.

Thus, Lord, I implore you to give me grace and, that in thy footsteps, with the house of my sensuality and the kingdom of my vices and sins behind, I may make of all things an occasion to serve thee and hold to the holy commandments so that the practice of observing them may instruct me further; that by simply reading and becoming familiar with them I may find the good of your grace for my soul, and thus, as I am secure in the belief that thy service is loving and gentle I render thee thanks that thou hast taken me under thy cloak, free from the errors into which I see and have seen so many people walk into now, on the road to Hell. And this is such an agony that I do not know whose heart it would not tear apart to see the terrible suffering and aweful grief of these idol worshipers whom the devil has always led, and continues to lead, to Hell. And if this is evil on the part of the devil, who attempts and achieves this, then God must permit it, so that if men do not wish to be guided by the light of reason that he has bestowed upon them, they begin to be tormented in this life and to feel part of the Hell they deserve in the difficult rites they continually perform to the demon god, with lengthy fasts, vigils and abstinence, with unbelievable offerings and gifts of their possessions and property, with the constant shedding of their own blood, with severe pain and wounds to their bodies and, what is worse and more serious, with the lives of their fellows and brothers. Yet with all this, the demon is never satiated or satisfied with their torments and labors, nor with leading them into hell through them, where he keeps them in eternal torment. Truly, God is more easily appeased, and is satisfied with less torment and death, for did he not cry out to the great patriarch Abraham that he should stay his hand against taking the life of his son, because his Majesty had determined to send his own son into the world and to let him lose his life on the cross, so that men should see that for the son of eternal God the command of his Father is weighty, though it be to him most sweet and only apparently a burden to man.

Therefore, let men cast out faintness from their hearts and their fear of the work of this holy law of God, for the weight of it is an illusion and it soon becomes balm to the body and soul. This all the more since, besides it being right for God to be well served and this we owe to him in just payment of our debt, all is for our benefit not only eternal but also temporal. Then let all us Christians, especially priests, understand that in this life it is a great shame and disgrace, and in the life to come it shall be greater, to see that the demon finds men to serve him with unbelievable labors only to go, in reward for them, to hell, but that God can find hardly any man to serve him faithfully, obeying his gentle commandments, and so go to eternal glory.

Therefore you, priest of God, tell me if you have taken heed of the office of these unhappy priests of the demon and of all those that in the holy Scriptures we find were such in ancient times, how much more laborious, long and frequent their fasts were than yours; how much more constant they were in their vigils and miserable prayers than you; how much more careful and painstaking in their duties than you are in yours; with how much more zeal than you they understood how to teach their foul doctrines. And if with this you find yourself in any error, correct it and remember that you are a priest of the Lord on high and that this office alone obliges you to seek to live in purity and righteouness, the purity of and angel rather than of a man.

XLIV

The products of the land

Yucatán is a land with the least soil I have seen, for it is all flat living rock and the earth is so curiously thin that there must be few places

Harvesting corn.

where it is possible to dig down seven feet without coming upon great banks of very large rocks. This stone is not very good for delicate work because it is hard and coarse, but even so it has served for making the great number of buildings that there are in that country. The land is very good for lime, of which there is much, and it is wonderful how fertile the soil is on top of or between the stones.

All that grows in this country grows better and more abundantly among the rocks than on open ground, because on the open ground that there sometimes is no trees grow, and the Indians do not sow their crops on it; there is nothing but grass. But among the rocks and on top of them they sow, and all their crops grow and all the trees flourish, some so large and beautiful that they are a wonder to see. The reason for this I believe to be that there is more moisture, and it is retained better, among the stones than on open ground.

Until now, no kind of native metal has been found in this land, and it is amazing that without it so many buildings have been constructed, for the Indians can give no information about the tools that were used. But since they had no metals, God provided a range of hills of pure flint near the range crossing the country that I told of in the first chapter. From this they obtained stones of which they fashioned the points of war spears and the knives they used for sacrifices (of which the priests had a goodly store); they used to make, and still make, the tips of arrows from it, and thus the flint served them as metal. They had a certain pale-colored brass with a little gold in it; this they cast into hatchets, the little rattling bells they wore when dancing, and a sort of small chisel which they used in making idols and hollowed out blow-pipes, like the figure in the margin, for they used the blowpipe a great deal and are good shots. This brass and other plaques or sheets of harder metal were brought by the people of Tabasco to trade for the products of Yucatán for their idols. There was no other type of metal among these people.

According to the wise, one of the things most necessary to human life is water, so much so that without it the land cannot produce its fruits or man live. Yucatán lacks the great numbers of rivers to be found in neighboring countries, having only two. One of these is the Río Lagartos, which flows into the sea at a headland, and the other is the Campotón, both brackish, with bad water, so God provided many sources of very fine water, some natural and some specially created.

Nature worked so differently in this country in the matter of rivers and springs that the waters that in the rest of the world flow above ground, here all run under the earth in hidden channels. We have been shown that almost all the coast is full of freshwater springs that rise in the sea, and in many places water can be taken from them (as I have done mysel) when the shore is left dry by the ebb tide.

Inland, God has provided some deep hollows in the rock, which the Indians call *zenotes*, that drop with sheer sides down to the water. In some of them there are furious currents that have been known to carry away cattle that fall into them. All these currents flow out into the sea and create the springs mentioned above.

These *zenotes* contain very fine water and are a sight worth seeing, for some of them have sheer rock side down to the water and others have some mouths that God created or were caused by the lightning that often strikes, or by other accidents. Inside there are handsome vaults of living rock and on the surface trees, so that above is forest and below, the *zenotes*. There are some where a caravel could be taken and sailed, and others larger or smaller. Those people who could took their water from these wells, those who could not dug their own wells, but since they did not have the tools for this purpose, they were very poor ones. But now we have given them not only the means to make good wells but also pump wells with storage tanks from which they take their water as if from the springs.

There are also lagoons, but all of them have brackish water that is too foul to drink, and they do not flow freely, as the *zenotes* do. This country has a remarkable thing in the matter of wells, and this is that wherever the ground is dug into good spring water gushes up. Some of these are so good that a spear can be sunk into them, and wherever wells have been dug, at half a man's height above the water level has been found a layer of seashells of many different types and colors, both large and small, like those that are on the seashore, and sand that has turned into hard, white rock. At *Maní*, the town of the king, we dug a deep shaft to make a bucket well for the Indians, and when we had gone down some seven or eight fathoms into the solid rock we discovered a tomb a good seven feet long filled with very fresh bright-red earth and human bones, and all of them were almost turned to stone. There were still two or three fathoms to go before reaching water, and before there was a vault created by God in such a way that the tomb was enclosed in the rock and it was possible to walk underground to where the water lay. We could not understand how this had come about, ecept by supposing that the grave had been dug there from the inside, and afterwards, with the moisture of the cave and the passage of time the rock grew around it and hardened, sealing up the tomb.

As well as the two rivers that I have said there are in this country, there is a spring three leagues from the sea, near Campeche that is saline, and in the whole country there is no other, nor other waters.

The Indians who live near the hills, because their wells are very deep, have the custom of making basins in the rock to collect water for their homes in the rainy season, because at that time there are heavy downpours, sometimes with a lot of thunder and lightning. All these wells, particularly those near the sea, rise and fall with the tide each day, which shows clearly that all of them are the waters of rivers that run underground to the sea.

There is a marsh worthy of mention in Yucatán that is over seventy leagues long and entirely saline. It begins on the coast of *Ekab*, which is near the Isla de Mujeres, and runs very close to the seashore, between it and the forest until it almost reaches Campeche. It is not deep because there is so little space for it, but it is bad to cross when traveling from the towns to the coast or vice versa because of the trees and great quantity of mud. This marsh is so saline that God has there created some of the finest salt I have seen in my life; when ground, it is very white, and those who know say that it is so good that half a peck of it salts more than a whole peck from other places. Our Lord brings forth the salt of this marsh from rainwater, not from the sea, which does not enter it because between it and the sea there is a strip of land that runs the whole length of it, separating it from the sea. Thus, in the rainy season this marsh becomes swollen with water, and the salt clumps together into large and small lumps that look like sugar candy, no less. Four or five months after the rains, when the lagoon has dried up somewhat, the Indians formerly used to go to gather the salt, taking the lumps from the water and carrying them off to dry. They had their special places for this marked in the lagoon that were the richest in salt and had less mud and water. They would not go gathering salt without leave of the chiefs who had most right to it because they lived nearby. All those who came for salt gave a small tribute to these chiefs, either of the salt itself of things from their own regions. A leading man named Francisco Euan, from the town of Caucel gave evidence of this custom, and also proved that the authorities of the town of Mayapán had settled his ancestors on the coast to take charge of the area and the distribution of salt, and therefore the Audiencia of Guatemala ordered those who went to collect salt in his district to give him the same tribute today. Much salt is now gathered in its time of year to be taken to Mexico, Honduras and Havana. In some parts this marsh produces fine fish and, though they are not large, they have an excellent flavor.

XLV

The fish in Yucatán

Not only are there fish in the lagoon, but also along the coast, in such abundance that the Indians pay little attention to those of the lagoon, except for those who do not have a supply of nets, and these hunt the fish with arrows, spearing many because the water is shallow. Others net great quantities of fish that they either eat or else sell throughout the region.

Fishing.

They either salt or sun-dry the fish without salt, and they know which of these processes is suited to each kind of fish. The sun-dried fish keeps for many days and is taken to twenty or thirty leagues for sale. To eat it, they cook it again, and it is tasty and wholesome.

The fish on that coast that they catch are gray mullet, plump and very good; a fish like a trout as to color, speckles and flavor but that are fatter, and good eating, which in their language is *uzcay*. There are very good sea bass, sardines and also flounder, Spanish mackerel, moharras and an infinite variety of smaller fish. There is very good octopus on the coast of Campeche, and three or four sorts of dogfish that are very good and wholesome, especially one kind that are wonderfully plump and have very different heads from the others for they are round and amazingly flat; they have their mouths on the undersides and their eyes on the edges of the round part. These they call *alipechpol*. They also catch some very large fish that look like mantas, which they cut up and preserve in salt. It dies all around the edges of the lagoon and is very good, but I do not know if this fish is skate.

There are many manatees on the coast between Campeche and La Desconocida which, apart from the large amount of fish-flesh or meat that they have on them produce a great deal of fat that is excellent for cooking foods. Wonderful things are told of these manatees; in particular the author of the "General History of the Indies" relates that on the island of Hispaniola an Indian chief had one of them in a lake that was so well-trained that it would come to the shore when called by its given name, which was "Matu." What I can say about them is that they are so large that much more meat can be taken from them than from a good sized calf, and a quantity of fat. They breed like land animals, and for this they have male and female parts. The female always gives birth to two young, no more, no less, and does not lay eggs as do other fish. They have two flippers like strong arms with which they swim; the face looks very much like that of an ox, and they lift out of the water to graze on shore plants. Bats often bite them on their rounded flat snouts and they die of this because they bleed profusely from any cut. The meat of them is good, especially when it is fresh; with mustard it tastes almost like good beef. The Indians kill them with harpoons in the following manner: they look for them in shallows and low water (for this is a fish that cannot swim deep), taking with them their harpoons attached to ropes with floats on the ends. When they find them they shoot them with the harpoon and set free the lines and floats with them. They try to escape from the pain of the wounds by swimming hither and thither in the shallows; they never go into the depths of the sea because they do not know how. As they are so large they stir up the mud as they move, and since they bleed so much they soon bleed t death. Using the trail of mud, the Indians follow them in their boats, find them with the floats and take them. This fish is good sport and highly appreciated because it is all flesh and fat.

There is another fish on this coast that they call *ba*, which is broad and round and makes good eating, but it is very dangerous to catch or to find. This does not go into deep water either and is fond of swimming in the muddy shallows where the Indians shoot it with their bows and arrows; but if they are careless walking near it, or step on it in the water, it straightway attacks with its tail, which is long and thin, and inflicts a wound with a saw it has on it so ferociously that it cannot be removed from where it enters without making the wound much larger, because the teeth point backwards, as is shown here. The Indians used these small saws for cutting their flesh in the sacrifices to the evil god, and it was the responsability of the priests to keep them, and they had many, They are very dainty, for they are of white bone curiously formed like a saw, just as sharp and delicate, that cuts like a knifeblade.

There is a small fish which is so poisonous that no one who eats it fails to swell up and die very quickly. It deceives neople many times, although it is well known, because it takes some time to die out of the water, swelling up greatly. There are very fine oysters in the Campotón river and many sharks along all the coast.

XLVI

Iguanas and alligators

In addition to the fish living in the waters there are other creatures that use and inhabit both water and land, such as the many iguanas, which are like the lizards of Spain in shape, size and color, though they are not so green. These lay large numbers of eggs and are always found near the sea or where there is water. They live in water or on land indifferently, which is why the Spaniards eat them in times of fast and find them exceptional and wholesome food. There are so many of these that they supply everybody in Lent. The Indians hunt them with lassos as they lie high in the trees or in holes of trees. It is incredible how they can go without food, for after they have been caught they sometimes live for twenty or thirty days without eating a mouthful and without growing thin. I have heard for a fact that if their bellies are rubbed with sand they grow very fat. The dung of these animals is an excellent remedy for clouds in the eyes, applied to them when it is fresh.

There are wonderfully great turtles, some of them much bigger than large, round shields, and they are good eating, with a large amount of flesh. They lay eggs the size of a hen's, but 150 or 200, making a large hole in the beach, away from the water and then covering them with sand; here the baby turtles hatch out. There are other kinds of turtles on land, in the dry country and in the lagoons.

I have sometimes seen a fish on the coast that, as it is completely covered in a shell I left to mention here. It is, then, the size of a small turtle, covered above by a delicate, round shell of a beautiful shape and very pale green. It has a tail of the same shell, so slender that it

An guana.

looks like a gimlet and some six inches long. On the underside it has many legs and is all full of tiny eggs; there is nothing edible of it save the eggs, and the Indians eat them in quantity. They call this creature *mex* in their language.

There are very fierce alligators which, though they usually keep to the water, come out and stay on the land for long periods. They either eat on land or with their heads out of the water because they have no gills and are not able to chew in the water. It is a heavy animal that does not stray far from water, but it has amazing speed in attacking anything or in fleeing. It is ready to eat anything, and strange things are told of it; what I know myself is that one killed one of our Indians as he was bathing in a lagoon near a monastery. Then a friar quickly went with the Indians to kill it, and to kill it they took a smallish dog and drove a stout pointed stake through it from mouth to tail. Then they fastened a very strong rope round the middle of the dog and threw it into the lake. The alligator appeared immediately, seized it between its teeth, and swallowed it. When it had been swallowed, those who were with the friar pulled on the rope and with great effort and difficulty dragged the alligator out as the stake turned inside its body. On opening it they found half of the man inside its belly as well as the little dog. These alligators breed like land animals, but lay eggs, for which they dig a large hole in the sand very close to the water. They lay three hundred and more eggs, which are larger than birds' eggs, and leave them there until the time when nature has taught them that they are ready to hatch, then they come back to the place and wait. The young alligators hatch out in this manner: they emerge from the egg as large as the palm of a hand and wait for a wave to break close to them and when they feel it they throw themselves into the water. All those which miss it die on the sand, for since they are so tender and the sand so very hot from the sun, they dry up and die immediately. Those that reach the water all survive and begin to swim in all directions until their parents appear, and then they follow them. This is why very few live despite so many eggs being laid, not without the work of the divine providence that desires that there should be more of the things that are beneficial to us than of those which are harmful and could do so much injury, like these beasts if they were all to live.

XLVII

How there are serpents and other venomous animals

Of snakes or serpents there is a geat variety of many colors and they are not dangerous save two kinds that are very poisonous and much larger than those here in Spain. They call these *taxinchan*. There are other very venomous ones that are very long, with a rattle on the tail. Othe very large ones that can swallow a rabbit or two, but are not harmful; in fact, there are Indians who easily take hold of both kinds without being harmed.

There is a sort of lizard, larger than those here, of which the Indians are terribly afraid because, they say, when it is touched it produces a sweat that is deadly poison. There are many scorpions among the rocks, but they are not as poisonous as those here in Spain. There is a type of large ant whose bite is much worse than that of the scorpions because it causes more pain and inflammation, and the inflammation lasts more than twice as long as that from a scorpion, as I know from experience.

There are two sorts of spiders: one is very small and foul-smelling, the other is very large and all covered with very fine black spines that look like hair and hold the poison. The Indians ae very careful not to touch them where there are any.

There is a small, red grub from which a yellow ointment is made that is very good for swellings and sores, simply by beating or crushing them togehter. It also serves for oil in painting vessels, and makes the paint strong.

XLVIII

Of the bees and their honey and wax

There are two kinds of bees and both are much smaller than ours. The larger of them live in hives, which are very small. They do not build honeycombs like ours do but make some small sacs of wax about te size of a walnut, all close together and full of honey. To collect the honey the Indians simply open the hive and break the sacs with a stick so the honey runs out, and they take the wax when they wish. The others live in the woods, in the hollows of trees and rocks, and there are to be found the wax and honey that abound in this country. The honey is very good, except that because the plants on which the bees feed are very lush, it is rather thin and watery and must be boiled up on the fire, and with this it becomes very good and long-lasting. The wax is good save for being very smoky;; the reason for this has never been discovered. In some districts it is much yellower because of the flowers. These bees do not sting or do any harm when the honey is gathered.

XLIX

The flora of Yucatán

The variety of plants and flowers that embellish Yucatán in their seasons on both trees and plants is great and most remarkable. Many of them are wonderfully delicate and beautiful, with different colors and scents and these, as well as dressing the woods and fields in beauty also provide very abundant food for the bees for their honey and wax. I shall here mention some of them, both for their lovely perfume and beauty and for the good use to which the inhabitants of these lands put them.

There is wormwood, much leafier and aromatic than what we have here, and with longer and narrower leaves; the Indians grow it for the scent and for pleasure, and I have noticed that the plants grow better when the Indian women put ashes at the foot.

There is a plant with very broad leaves and tall, thick branches that is paricularly fresh and fertile, growing very easily from cuttings in the same profusion as osiers, though they cannot be compared in any way. If a leaf is rubbed gently between the hands it has a real smell of clover, although it loses it when it is dry. It is very good for keeping the temples fresh at festivals and is used for this.

There is so much swet basil that the countryside if full of it in some places, and growing among rocks it is very fresh, beautiful and scented, though it does not compare with that grown in gardens, taken from here, which grows and spreads wonderfully.

There is a flower that they call *tixzula*, with the most delicate perfume I have ever smelled, much more so than jasmine; it is white, and there is also mauve, and since it grows from fat bulbs it could be brought to Spain. It is like this: the bulbs put forth tall, thick and very green sword-shaped leaves that last all year, and once a year they put up a green stem at the center, some three fingers broad and as thick and long as the leaves. At the top of this stem the flowers grow in a group, each one about six inches long with its stalk. They are open, with five long flat petals joined at the base by a delicate white membrane. In the center they have some little yellow webs, and these yellow and white flowers are remarkably beautiful. When the stalk is cut and placed in a jug of water it keeps its delicate perfume for many days because the flowers do not open together but little by little.

There are some small, very white and fragant lilies that last a long time in water which would be easy to bring here because these also grow from bulbs. They are just like our Easter lilies, except that the scent is more delicate and does not make the head ache, and they do not have the yellow in the center that lilies have. There is a flower called *ixlaul* that I have been told is very pretty and very sweet.

There is also a kind of tree called *nicté* that bears many whithe flowers, some yellow and some purple at the center; these are very fresh and fragrant, and of them they make elegant posies, and those who so wish, electuary.

There is a flower they call *kom* that has a very strong scent that burns when it is smelled; it could easily be brought here. Its leaves are beautifully green and broad. As well as these sweet-smelling flowers and plants there are others that are very useful and medicinal, among them two sorts of nightshade that are very green and fine.

There is much scale fern and maidenhair fern and a plant whose leaves, boiled in water bring down swelling in the feet and legs marvellously. There is another that is very good for curing old sores which they call *iaxpalialché*. There is also another that tastes just like fennel and is very good eaten boiled and is good for curing sores, put on raw like the other plant. In the region of *Bac-halar* sarsaparilla is found.

They have a certain plant hat grows in wells and other places that is triangular like sedge, but much thicker, and of this they make their baskets. They usually dye the plant different colors, and make very fine baskets. They have a wild plant which they also grow near their houses, when it is better, from which they get a sort of hemp fiber that they use to make numberless useful articles. Also, in certain trees there is a plant that grows wild and produces fruit like small cucumbers; with these they make gums or glues for sticking together anything they need.

The crops they have for human consumption are: very good maize of many varieties and colors, which they harvest in great quantities and keep in cribs and grain-stores for lean years. There are two types of small beans, one black and the other of various colors; there is another, brought by the Spaniards, that is small and whitish.

They have their pepper. There are many different kinds of squash, some are for their seeds, that are taken out and used in cooking some dishes, others are to eat roasted or boiled, and others to make vessels for household use. They now have very good melons, and pumpkins, from Spain; we have set them to gathering millet, which is excellent food.

They have a wonderfully refreshing and delicious fruit that is cultivated, and the fruit is the root, which grows like a fat, white turnip; they are eaten raw with salt. The other cultivated root that grows under the earth and is very nutritious, has many varieties, there being purple, yellow and white. These are eaten boiled or roasted, and make very good eating; they taste rather like chestnuts and, roasted, help drinking. There are two other sorts of roots that serve the Indians as food. There are two other wild roots that resemble the first two I described which help the Indians in times of hunger, but otherwise they pay no heed to them.

They have a small tree with soft branches and a lot of sap, the leaves of which are eaten cooked. They taste like kale and are good with plenty of fat bacon. The Indians plant this as soon as they settle anywhere and have leaves to gather all the year. There is very good endive growing on their plots, but they never think of eating it.

It is reason to praise God together with the prophet who says "Admirable, o Lord, is thy name in all the earth" for the great number of trees that Thy Majesty has created in this country, all so different from ours that until today I have not seen one I know (I speak of Yucatán, for elsewhere I have), and both the Indians and the Spanish use and benefit from all of them.

There is a tree with whose fruit, which is like a round pumpkin, the Indians make their vessels; they are very good and they make them colorfully and attractively painted. Of this same type there is another that has a smaller, very hard fruit from which they make little containers for ointment and for other purposes.

There is another that bears a fruit like a hazelnut, with a pit that they use to make fine beads, and the shell they use as soap for washing clothes, making suds with it.

They took great care of the tree that gives incense for their demons, and this they extracted by cutting the bark f the tree with a stone so that the gum or resin would run out. It is a cool-looking tree, tall and with good shade and foliage, but the flower turns beeswax black wherever the tree grows. There is a tree that grows near the wells, beautifully tall with fresh green leaves. It is wonderful to see how the branches spread, growing in groups of three or more at regular intervals round the tree, and thus they continue to spread and the trunk to grow.

There are cedars, but not of the fine type. There is a kind of wood that is yellowish and veined like oak; it is marvelously strong and very hard and so tough that we found it the doorways of the buildings at Izamal, used as doorposts with all the weight of the building resting on them. There is another very strong wood of which they make bows and spears, and it is tawny colored. There is another, deep orange in color, with which they make staffs; it is very strong and I think its name is brazilwood.

There are many of the trees that they say are good for the buboes, which they call zon. Ther is a tree whose sap is poison and injures whatever it touches, and its shade brings disease, especially if one sleeps in it. There is another all covered with pairs of long, very hard and broad thorns on which no bird can settle or nest; it has some thorns that are all hollow inside and always full of ants. There is another tree of great height and size that bears fruit like carob beans full of black seeds like pine-nuts that the Indians eat in times of need, and with its roots they make buckets for drawing water from wells or tanks.

There are other trees whose bark the Indians use to make small vessels for taking water to drink, others from which they make rope, and yet others with whose mashed bark they make a liquid for polishing stucco surfaces that makes them very hard. Ther are very fine mulberry trees with good wood, and so many others trees that are useful and beneficial that it is amazing. In the fields and woods they have many different types of osiers from which they make all kinds of baskets and which they use for lashing together their houses and whatever else they need. The use they put this to is marvelous. There is a tree whose sap is an excellent remedy for setting loose teeth. There is another has a certain large fruit full of floss that is better for pillows than the tow of the Alcarria plateau in Spain.

Fearing to do less than justice to the fruits or their trees I decided to put them on their own. I shall speak first of the wine tree as it is something the Indians esteem highly and therefore almost all of them planted in their plots or around their houses. It is an ugly tree without any other use than to make wine from its roots together with honey and water. In this country there are certain wild vines with edible grapes; there are many on the coast of *Kupul*. There are plum trees with many different kinds of fruit, some of them very tasty and wholesome, but very different from ours, having little flesh and a large stane, contrary to the ones to be bought here. This tree puts out fruit before the leaves; it has no blossom, just the fruit. There are many bananas, which were introduced by the Spanish, for there were none here before. There is a very large tree that bears a large, rather long and fat fruit with red flesh that is very good to eat. It does not put out blossom, just the fruit itself, at first very small and growing very gradually. There is another very leafy and beautiful tree that never loses its leaves, and without producing a flower it gives a fruit that is as sweet or even sweeter than the one above. It is small, very tasty and delicious to eat, ad very delicate. Some are better than others, so good that they would be much appreciated here if we had them; in their language they are called *ya*. There is another very fine, fresh tree that never loses its leaves and bears some delicious little figs that they call *ox*. Another wonderfully fine tree has fruit like large eggs. The Indians gather them green and ripen them is ashes; when ripe it is lovely, as sweet and rich as egg-yolk. Another tree bears a yellow fruit too, not as large as the other, but softer and sweeter; after being eaten, this leaves a stone like a small, soft burr that is curious to see. There is another very green and beautiful tree that bears fruit exactly like hazelnuts with their husks; inside the husk is a fruit like a cherry with a large stone. The Indians call these *vayam* and the Spanish *guayas*. There is a fruit the Spanish introduced that is good to eat and wholesome called *guayaba*.

In the hills there are two kinds of trees. One bears fruit as large as a good pear, very green and thick-skinned; these they soften by beating them on a stone, then they have a very special flavor. The other bears very large fruit the shape of pine cones that is good eating, being juicy and acid; it has nany small pits, but these are not good. There is a tree that always grows in open places, never among other trees, but alone, whose bark is very good for tanning hides, like sumac. It bears a small, tasty, yellow fruit of which women are very fond. There is a very large, leafy tree that the Indians call *on*; it bears fruit like a small gourd, very soft, tasting like butter, and oily; it is very nourishing and satisfying. It has a large pit and a thin skin and is eaten cut into slices like melon, but with salt.

There are some very spiny and ugly thistles that grow in sections, always near other trees and mixed in with them. These bear a fruit shaped rather like an artichoke with red skin, easy to pick and without any spines. The flesh inside is white and full of tiny black seeds. It is wonderfully sweet and delicate and so juicy that it melts in the mouth; it is eaten in round slices, like and orange, and with salt. The Indians cannot find enough of them in the forests to satisfy the Spanish.

There is a spongy and ugly, though large tree that bears a sort of fruit full of delicious yellow flesh and coarse little pits like hempseeds but much bigger, which are good for the urine. Of this fruit they make a good preserve; the tree puts out leaves after the fruit is over. There is a small rather thorny tree that bears fruits like slender cucumbers, quite long. Its taste is somewhat like that of the cardoon and it is eaten in slices, with salt; the seeds are like those of a cucumber, many and tender. If this fruit comes to have a hole in it by any chance while it is on the tree, a sort of gummy substance collects in it whith the smell of fine civet. There is another tree whose blossoms are filled with soft perfume and whose fruit is what here in Spain is called "white-meat fruit", and there are many varieties of these trees, which bear either good or excellent fruit.

There is a small tree that the Indians grow near their houses that has burrs like chestnuts, but not so big or so prickly. They open when they are ripe and inside have some small seeds that they and even the Spanish use to give their cooked dishes a color like saffron gives. The color is so good that it stains heavily.

I am sure that there must be fruits I have omitted, but I shall now speak of those of the palm trees, of which there are two kinds. The fronds of one kind of palm are used to thatch houses, and these are very tall and slim and bear great bunches of a quite good black fruit like chickpeas of which the Indian women are very fond. The other palms are low and very thorny and their leaves, which are very short and sparse are of no use at all. They bear large bunches of round, green fruit as big as pigeons' eggs. When the skin is taken off there is a very hard stone, and this, broken open, yields a round kernel the size of a hazelnut that is very tasty and of use in times of bad harvests. With it they make the hot nourishment they drink in the morning and, in case of need, any dish could be cooked with milk made from it, which is like almond milk.

They pick an amazing amount of cotton, which grows in all parts of the country and of which there are two sorts: the first is sown every year and the bush does not last for more than that year: it is very small. The bush of the other lasts for five or six years and in every one produces its fruits, which are pods the size of walnuts with green husks that open out into four parts in due season, and there is the cotton.

Cochineal also used to be collected, and they say that it was the best in the Indies because it was dry country; the Indians still gather a little in some places.

Color there are of many kinds, dyes made from certain trees and flowers, but because the Indians do not know how to refine them with gums to give them the temper they need so as not to change, they fade. But those who gather the fiber have found remedies that they say will give results as good as the best anywhere.

L

Birds of the land and of the sea

The abundance of birds that this country has is amazingly great, and they are so varied that he who filled these lands with them as if in blessing, is much to be praised. They have poultry, such as large numbers of native hen and cock birds that they raise in their hoses, although they are troublesome. They have begun to raise birds from Spain, hens, which thrive in large numbers, and there are chickens from them at all times of the year. They raise tame pigeons like ours, and these breed much. They raise a certain type of large, white ducks for their down, and I think these came to them from Peru; they pluck their breasts frequently and use these feathers for embroidering their clothes.

There are many different kinds of birds, and many of them are very handsome. Among them there are two types of very pretty little turtle doves; one kind is very small, easy to raise and tame. There is a small bird that has a song as sweet as the nightingale has which they call

A turkey.

ixyalchamil; it frequents the walls of houses that have gardens and in the trees of these. There is another large, very handsome bird, very dark green in color, that has only two long feathers in its tail, and no others even half the length, with down at the ends; it lives in buildings and goes about only in the mornings. There are other birds that in their mschievousness and bodies are like magpies, and they scream out at people as they pass by, not letting them move secretly. There are many little swifts or swallows, but I think they are swifts because they do not nest on houses as swallows do. There is a large, handsome bird of many colors that has a big, very strong beak, which keeps to dry, rotten trees, holding on with its claws and making holes in the hard bark with its beak, pecking so loudly that it can be heard from a good distance away, to extract the grubs it lives on from the wood. These birds make so many holes that the trees where these grubs are to be found are riddled like a sieve from top to bottom.

There are many birds in the countryside, all god to eat, including three sorts of pretty little pigeons. There are some birds just like the partidges of Spain except that they have very long legs, but red and they make very poor eating; however they are wonderfully tame if raised in the house. There are many fine quail that are a little bigger than ours and very good eating. They fly little, and the Indians hunt them with dogs as they perch in the trees, throwing a lasso around their necks. It is very fine sport. There are many brownish speckled pheasants of quite good size, but not so good to eat as those from Italy. There is a bird the size of the native poultry that they call *cambul* which is really handsome, very bold and good to eat. Another there is that they call *cox*, as large as the other that walks and moves about furiously. The maeles are jet black all over, with fine crests of curled feathers and handsome yellow eyelids. There are many peacocks and their plumage, though not so beautiful as that of those here in Spain, is nevertheless very attractive. The birds are handsome, as big as the cock birds of the Indians and just as good to eat.

The Indians shoot all the large birds with arrows amongst the trees; they steal the eggs of all them, give them to their hen-birds to hatch, and so they grow up very tame. There are three of four types of large and small parrots, and so many flocks of them that they do much damage to the crops.

There are other birds that are nocturnal, such as barn owls, little owls and nightjars; it is amusing to walk at night because long stretches of the road ahead can be seen taking flight at the approach of people. They trouble the Indians greatly, since they consider them birds of ill omen, as they do others.

There are some very carnivorous birds that the Spanish call *auras* and the Indians *kuch*, which are black and have a head and neck like the native poultry's and a longish hooked beak. They are very squalid, and almost always to be found near stables and latrines, eating filth and looking for carrion to feed upon. It is a fact that no nest of theirs has yet been found nor any knowledge of where they breed, and for this reason some people say that they live for two hundred years or more, while others that they are really crows. They can smell dead flesh so keenly that the Indians, to trace deer that they have shot at and have run away wounded have no answer but to climb a tall tree and look where these birds are gathering; there they are sure to find their prey.

There is a wonderfully wide variety of birds of prey, for there are small eagles, most handsome goshawks that are great hunters, and fine sparrow hawks as large as those here in Spain. There are lanners, gerfalcons and others that, not being a falconer, I do not recollect.

By the sea there is a wonderful, infinite variety and multitude of birds, and they are all beautiful in their own way. There are some as large as ostriches, but brown and having a larger bill. They keep to the water, hunting for fish, and when they see a fish they rise into the airand then swoop down to scoop it up into their great bill and crop. They never srike in vain, and after striking remain swimming and swallowing the fish alive without preparing or scalimg it at all.There are some large slender birds that fly at a very great height that have a forked tail and their fat is an excellent remedy for the scars of cuts and for numbness in the limbs as a result of wounds. There are some ducks that can stay under water for a very long time to fish their food; they are very quick and have a hook on their beaks for catching fish. There are some other beautiful little ducks called *maxix*; they are very tame and are raised in houses and have no notion of running away.

There are many sorts of large and small herons –gray or white, large or small. In the Laguna de Términos there are many pale scarlet ones like the color of powdered cochineal, and so many sorts of large and small birdlife that their number and variety is an amazing sight. It is even more interesting to see them all diligently searching for food on the shore, some entering the water after the waves break and then retreating, others hunting for food at the edge, and some robbing it from others by reaching it first. But what is most admirable is to see how God provide for all of them and has filled them with his blessing.

LI

Other animals in Yucatán

Many animals have been wanting to the Indians; in particular they have been without those most useful to man. They had others, however, that they used as food. None of these was domesticated save the dogs. These could not bark and would never hurt, but knew how to hunt, treeing quail and other birds and tracking deer, for some of them are great trackers. They are small and the Indians used to eat them at festivals, but I do believe that now they are ashamed of this and consider it a sign of proverty to eat them. They are said to have had a very good taste.

A tapir.

There are tapirs in only one small area behind the Campeche hills; there are many, and the Indians have told me that they are several colors of them, gray, dappled, bay, chestnut and some very white ones and some black. They keep more to this part of the country than to any other because it is an animal that is very fond of water and here there are many lakes among the woods and hills. They are as big as an ordinary sized mule, very agile, with cloven hooves like oxen and a short trunk in which they hold water. The Indians regard killing them as a great feat of courage, and the skin or parts of it was kept for generations as a memento, as I myself have seen.They call them *tzimin*, and have given horses the same name after them.

There are small lions and tigers, which the Indians hunt with bow and arrow as they lie in the trees. There is a certain kind of bear that is extremely fond of taking honey from the nests of bees. It is brown, with a few black patches, long in the body, short in the legs, and round-headed.

There is a type of wild goat, small, very light-footed, and rather dark in color. There are pigs, small animals that are very different from ours, since they have their navel on their backs and stink badly. There are amazing numbers of deer; they are small and the meat makes good eating. Of rabbits there is an infinite number, like ours in everything

A deer.

except the nose, which is long and not blunt at all, but like a sheep's; they are large and very good to eat.

There is a little animal that is very darkness-loving by nature, always keeping to caves and hiding places and going about at night. To hunt in that Indians set a special trap for it, where it is caught. It is similar to the hare, moving in leaps and bunched up. It has very long, narrow front teeth, a tail even smaller than a hare's and is very dark gold in color; it is wonderfully tame and friendly and is called *zub*.

There is another small animal, like a newly born piglet with the same little feet and the snout, and a great rooter. This is covered with scales so that is looks like nothing less than an armour-covered horse, with only the ears and paws showing, and even its neck and head covered with scales; it is tender and very good eating.

There are some other creatures like small dogs; they have a head shaped like a pig's and a long tail and are smoky gray in color, and so slow-moving that the Indians often catch them by the tail. They are predatory and move around the houses at night and no fowl escapes them eventually. The females gives birth to fourteen or eighteen young, like little weasels, without any covering of hair at all and extremely slow-moving. God has provided the mothers with a curious pocket on the belly where they can shelter them, for a flap of skin extends the

A jaguar.

whole length of the belly on each side and over the teats; and when the mother brings one side together with the other, the teats are covered, and when she wishes she opens the pocket and each of the young takes a teat in its mouth. When each of them has taken hold the mother closes these sides or flaps over them and presses them together so tightly that not one of them falls out. Thus laden, she goes about in search of food. She cares for them like this until they have fur and can move about.

There are foxes, just like the ones here except that they are not so big and do not have such fine tails. There is an animal that they call *chu* that is extremely mischievous, the size of a small dog, with a snout like a suckling pig. The Indian women raise them, and nothing can be left in their reach that they do not root into and upset. It is marvelous to see how fond they are of playing with the Indian women, searching for their lice and always running to them; but they have a mortal horror of men. There are many of these and they always go about together in single file, one behind the other, with their snouts tucked under the tail of another. They do much damage to the maize fields they get into.

There is a little animal like a squirrel, whit and banded whith dark yellow that is called *pay*, and this defends itself against those who follow or hurt it by urinating, and what it releases has such a terrible stink that nobody can stand it, and nothing on which it falls can ever be used again. I have been told that this stuff is not urine but a substance it secretes in a pouch under its tail. Whatever it is, this weapon protects it and the Indians kill one only by a miracle. There are many lovely squirrels, also moles and weasels, and many mice like those of Spain except for having very long noses.

LII

Conclusion

The Indians have not lost, but rather have gained much by the arrival of the Spaniards, for even in the least of matters it is still much, and many of the things that in time they will surely come to enjoy are increasing, and they are already beginning to appreciate and use many of them. There are already many good horses and many mules both male and female. Asses do not do well, and I believe that this is because of treating them well, because they are hardy beasts without fail and comfort harms them. There are many fine cows, many pigs, rams, ewes, goats and those of our dogs that earn their keep, all of which have come to be numbered among useful things in the Indies. Cats are very useful and necessary there, and the Indians are very fond of them.

Hens and pigeons; oranges, limes, citrons, grapes, pomegranates, figs, guavas and dates, bananas, melons and most vegetables have been brought here. Only melons and pumpkins grow from their own seeds, for the rest, fresh seed must be brought from Mexico. Silk is now being produced and it is very good.

Metal tools and the use of mechanical devices have been introduced, being well-received. The use of coins and of many other things from Spain they have, and although the Indians had done without these and could have continued to do so, with them they live incomparably more like civilized beings. They have more help in their labors and in the lightening of them because, in the words of the philosopher, art aids nature.

God, through our nation of Spain, has given the Indians not only the benefit of these things that are so necessary in the service of man and for which alone, whatever the Indians give now or will give to the Spanish, they will never pay, but they have received without payment things that can neither be bought nor deserved: the Christian justice and peace in which they now live. For these they owe more to Spain and its people, and mainly to their most Catholic monarchs —who with such constant care and such great Christianity have provided and still provide these two things— than to their first makers, evil fathers who begot them in sin and as sons of wrath, while Christianity creates them in grace and to enjoy eternal life. Their first founders did not know how to give guidance so that they would be free from the so many and so great errors in which they have lived. Justice has delivered them from these errors through preaching, and it must guard them against returning, and if they do return it must draw them away.

Rightly then can Spain glorify in God, since He chose her among other nations for the salvation of so many peoples, and therefore they owe her much more than to their founders or begetters; for as the blessed St. Gregory says, little benefit would it be to us to be born if we were not come to be redeemed by Christ our Lord. We can also say with Anselm, "What profit is it to us to be redeemed if we do not attain the fruit of redemption, which is our salvation?" Thus, those who say that because the Indians have suffered wrongs and ill-treatment from the Spanish and have received bad examples it would have been better not to have discovered them are in great error, for greater were the wrongs and ill-treatment they were perpetually meting out to one another, killing, taking slaves and sacrificing themselves to the evil gods. As for the bad example, if they have received any, or are given any now from some people, the king has repaired this, and repairs it every day with his justices and with the constant preaching and persevering opposition of the monastic orders to those who set or have set them. And in as much as the doctrine is evangelical, bad examples and offenses are necessary, and I believe they have been so among these people, so that they might learn, by separating the gold from the dross and the wheat from the chaff, how to esteem virtue, as they have indeed done by seeing, like the philosopher, that virtues shine out among vices, and the virtuous amongst the wicked. He who has given them bad example or offense has, alas, terrible punishment if he does not atone for them with some good.

And you, beloved reader, on your part pray to God that it might be so, and accept this my humble effort, pardoning its defects and remembering, when you come upon them, that not only do I not defend them (as St. Augustine relates that Tully would say of himself that he had never uttered a word that he would wish to retract, which did not please the saint because to err is human), but at the beginning, even before you meet them, you will find them revoked or confessed in my introductions or prologues. And thus you will judge, as did the blessed Augustine in his letter to Marcella, the difference between the man who confesses his error of fault, and the man who defends it. And you shall pardon mine as, according to the prophet, God pardons mine and yours, saying, "Lord, I swore that I would confess my ills and my failings, and forthwith thou hast pardoned them.".

The historian of the things of the Indies, to whom much is due for his work and for the light he shed on them, when writing of the affairs of Yucatán says that they used slings and spears hardened in fire in warfare. I have told of the the items that the Indians used in war and I do not wonder that to Francisco Hernández de Córdova and Juan de Grijalva the rocks that the Indians loosed at them seemed to be from slings when they were forced out of Champotón. But they do not throw with the sling, nor even do they know it, though they do throw stones most accurately and violently, aiming at their target with the left arm and their index finger. He says that there are hares: of course these are the animals described in paragraph four of chapter LI. He says that there are partridges, and what kind and sort they are; these you will find in paragraph I of chapter L.

Our historian also says that at Cape Cotoch crosses were found among the dead and the idols, and that he does not believe this to be true because if they were of the Spaniards who sailed from Spain and were then lost, they would certainly have reached other lands first, of which there are many. This I do not believe, and not for the reasoning that does not convince me; I do not believe it because we do not know what other places they could have sighted and where they might have landed before they came to Yucatán, or whether they did indeed reach land or not before arriving in Yucatán. But the reason why I do not believe this is that when Francisco Hernández and Grijalva reached Cotoch they did not set themselves to digging up the dead but to searching for gold among the living. Also, such I believe to be the virtue of the cross and the evil of the devil that he would not be able to endure seeing a cross amongst the idols for fear that one day its virtue would shatter them by miracle and would banish and confound him as the ark of the convenant did Dagon though it was not sanctified by the blood of the Son of God and graced by his holy limbs as was the sacred cross.

But as well as all this, I will relate what I was told by an Indian chief, a man of very good judgment and great repute. As we spoke of this subject one day I asked him if he had ever before heard tell of Christ our Lord or of his Cross, and he said in reply that he had never heard anything from his forefathers about Christ or the Cross, but that as they were tearing down a small building on a certain part of the coast, he and others had found in some graves, on the corpses and bones, some small metal crosses. They had not given any thought to the crosses until now, when they had beome Christians and saw it being worshiped and adored, and thus had supposed that those that had been buried there must have been Christians. If this was so, it is possible that some few people arrived from Spain and perished soon afterwards, which is why there is no memory of them left.

Printed in:
Programas Educativos S.A. de C.V.
Calz. Chabacano No.65 Local A
Col. Asturias
06850 – México, D.F. September 2009
Empresa Certificada por el ISO-9002